The Healing Presence

The Healing Presence

Photographs of the Sky and Children's Perceptions of Hope

A. J. Meek

Photographs by A. J. Meek

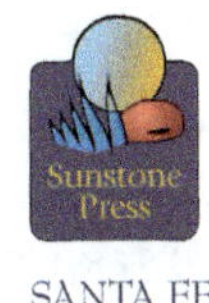

SANTA FE

Sunstone books may be purchased for educational, business, or sales promotional use. For information please write: Special Markets Department, Sunstone Press, P.O. Box 2321, Santa Fe, New Mexico 87504-2321.

Book and Cover design › Vicki Ahl
Body typeface › Bernard Modern Std
♾ Printed on acid-free paper

Library of Congress Cataloging-in-Publication Data

Meek, A. J.
[Photographs. Selections]
The healing presence : photographs of the sky and children's perceptions of hope / photographs by A.J. Meek.
pages cm
ISBN 978-0-86534-032-9 (softcover : alk. paper)
1. Photography of clouds. 2. Hope. 3. Imagery (Psychology) in children.
4. Children's writings. I. Title.
TR733.M44 2013
779--dc23

2013043967

WWW.SUNSTONEPRESS.COM
SUNSTONE PRESS / POST OFFICE BOX 2321 / SANTA FE, NM 87504-2321 /USA
(505) 988-4418 / ORDERS ONLY (800) 243-5644 / FAX (505) 988-1025

Dedicated to Michael Crespo

Artist, Colleague, and Friend
(1947–2010)

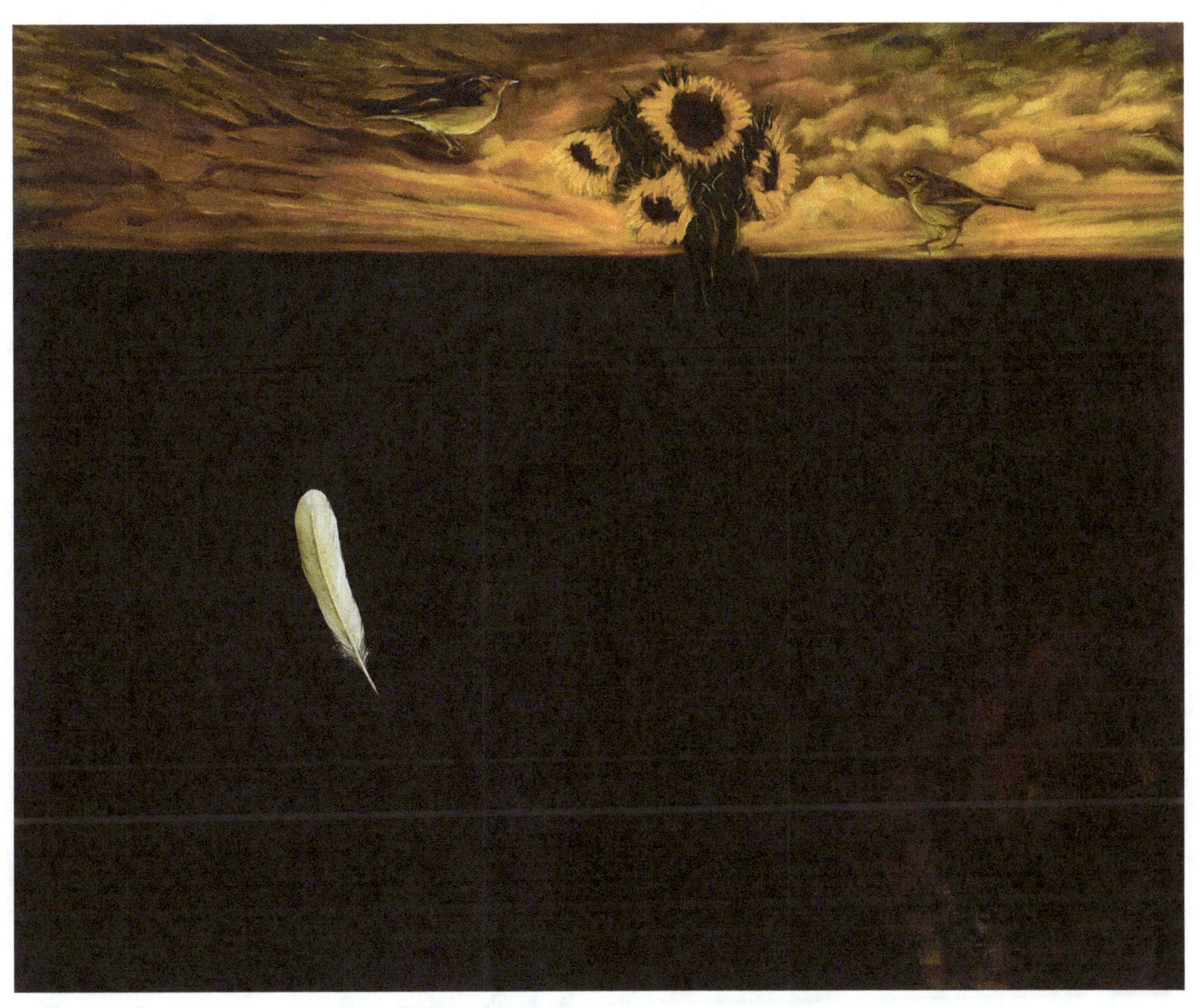

Untitled, Last Painting, Michael Crespo

CONTENTS

Preface

It was during meditation that the inspiration to pair children's poems and statements came to me. It was ways to communicate further the intention of my thesis, "The Healing Presence." I chose young people because, even though they have their own problems, they are resilient, honest, forthright and most don't yet have all the adult hang-ups and fears.

It was easy to enlist help from friends and family, children and grand children, but the rest was more difficult. I was lucky to find help in the form of a private school, English Literature teachers who made an assignment in their classes.

Photographs and text are independent of one another. I didn't want the children's perceptions to illustrate the photographs or visa versa. I find that this has the potential to weaken both. Instead, I asked participants to respond to keywords such as, Freedom, Light, Angels, God, Happiness, Peace, Friendship, or Courage. I then paired the statements with the photographs. These were translated into French as to better communicate internationally.

—A J Meek

Introduction

Do images heal? They do. That is the thesis of renowned photographer A. J. Meek with these photographs of the clouds paired with children's perceptions of hope.

"The feeling of freedom is exhilarating," Meek says in his photographer's comments for the work contain within. "The total package of sky and children's perception is designed to evoke a positive healing attitude within the viewer. When studied and meditated upon, the audience cannot maintain a negative thought."

Heavily influenced by Native American culture, these pictures, which were made in New Mexico and Louisiana, promote a feeling of well-being and inspiration. To be in the world but not of it is certainly the road less traveled and the most challenging for there are no earthly rewards for this choice—only peace.

He used a hand held 4 x 5 Crown Graphic camera to photograph the sky. The transparencies were processed in a commercial lab. Then the selection was scanned to create digital images, which could be printed.

Acknowledgements

I especially wish to thank the many children who submitted their poems for this project, as well as their teachers and parents who encouraged their participation. Special appreciation goes to Denise Magnat for her French translation of these poems, and to Clay Fourrier for his many hours working on the technical aspects of this book.

At the University of New Mexico, Dr. Rosalie Otero, Associate Dean of the Honors Program, for her positive influence; Jim Stone, Professor of Photography, for his encouragement when this work was at its infancy; the Art Department for their support in using their film loading labs; and poet David Wilde for the sharing of his work and his company at Albuquerque's El Patio and its famous #5 Chile Rellenos.

Photographer's Comments

The feeling of freedom is, for me, exhilarating. Nothing expresses that more than clouds. The clouds are constantly moving, being shifted by the winds, entertaining, and healing. The shapes are there and then they are not. I am reminded of sacred sand paintings, seen in ceremony and erased. However, I am a photographer. My job, to my way of thinking, is to reveal through the medium the invisible and to fix a place or a scene permanently in time and space for a potential viewer for a specific purpose—in this case, good intentions.

In 2009–2010 I spent time teaching in the Honors Program at the University of New Mexico in Albuquerque. It was a wonderful experience. I became influenced by the diversity of culture and for this sky project the Native American spirituality, nature and the voices of parallel worlds. One cannot help but be affected by such space—long and wide vistas where the earth touches the sky. It is said that sky is masculine and earth is feminine. Where they meet a creative power is released. The meaning of what makes a mountain or a place sacred is that it is so mysterious and beautifully inspiring that one cannot hold a negative thought when observed or meditated upon. Likewise, these photographs by their nature will promote a positive feeling and, therefore, evoke a shift or a healing energy within the viewer.

These images represent the divine light, the spiritual helpers, power animals, angels, bodhisattvas, and disciples.

As abstract patterns, more specific than spatters of paint on a flat surface or the random designs found in floor tiles, these pictures of clouds stand as portals into the world of shamanic wisdoms. They offer thoughts of freedom from the entrapment of suffering.

—AJM

Celtic Clouds

clouds fly like
gods in airy vaults
supreme above the
cliffs but nebulous too
of mist and dew
silhouette the blue
canvas called sky—
bony trees stand
in bold relief dead
as winter black as
coal—dim light
bright dawn brings
hope and altitude
brief glimpses of
paradise a celtic
dream too far
remote beyond
compare past
sleeping here
now— moving

7:30 –45 am, Monday, January 31, 2011
—David Wilde, Poet, New Mexico

The Prayer of Light

Light before me
Light behind me
Light at my left
Light at my right
Light above me
Light below me
Light unto me
Light in my surroundings
Light to all
Light to the universe

—Anonymous

For the Love of Clouds

I've looked at clouds from both sides now
From up and down, and still somehow
It's cloud illusions I recall
I really don't know clouds at all

—Joni Mitchell, 1969

In sacred art, which is not limited to iconology, there is an invitation into a deeper healing by entering light, space, and form. Finding the sacred is a process, and collaboration between imagery and viewer. By allowing art to open the psyche, there is a transcendent meeting point between creativity and universal oneness. Offered as a meditation, sacred images are a transmission of divine love. By incorporating these visual meditations into a daily practice, the viewer is better able to settle the mind to begin an inner journey into self-awareness. It is only in the contemplative practice that one is able to find a means to transmute suffering into joy, and thus sacred art has the capacity for profound healing.

Healing art is powerful because the imagery carries with it a higher frequency, not only in the colors, light, and form (form bound by sacred geometry, which mirrors the architectural universal principles), but also in the creative process itself. If open, the viewer is able to receive the intended benefits of the creative process. It is the intention(s) of the artist that can transmit the seeds of transformation. For hundreds of years, cloud imagery has been a powerful captivation for writers, painters, and more relatively recent, photographers. There is a rich photographic tradition from Edward Weston who photographed clouds in Mexico in the 1920s, to Alfred Stieglitz in his 1930s series called, "Equivalents," and to Ansel Adams in the great western landscape of the 1950s. These masterworks captured a single glorious moment of time. Contemporary photographers all across the world continue to work as subject the sublime nature of clouds.

Clouds provide a transcendent purity because they are both secular and sacred, not bound by human constructs. They are timeless, beyond mind, beyond religion. Clouds are the reminder that change is constant. When one takes the time to be in relationship with clouds, they teach us how to flow by not being attached to form. All shapes have a possible meaning and the possible meanings are infinite. By allowing ourselves to let go and relax, we return to our true nature, a state of bliss being. This is our Christ nature, our Bodhisattva, our Sat Nam. It is our immutable, timeless selves, our universal nature. Ironically, it is the immutable part of self that is able to transcend circumstance. When we get out of our cognitive constructs, losing ourselves so-to-speak, it makes room for the divine instant to rush in and fill our deeper psyche. It is in that moment that we are *filled*, able to receive unlimited joy. It is in that divine instant that we too become as timeless and as vast as the sky and as varied moment to moment as the clouds. We are whole.

Clouds help us return to that joy of knowing our inner self, and it is that joy that has the power to heal. Who of us does not recall the instant pleasure of being in one of nature's vast and varied rooms, staring out into the infinite sky, thankfully losing ourselves into mindlessness. Some of us may have been told to stop daydreaming, to "get your head out of the clouds." For a while, we learn to believe that we are better off to be outside of our illumined daydream. We essentially become separated into the struggles of productivity. Then some of us forget how assessable is our healing. We forget who we really are. Who we really are is met time and time again in the sacredness of the divine instant, in that space of *timelessness*. For the love of clouds, it is the cloud that knows that best.

—Patricia L. Meek, MFA, MA, LPC

If I were a horse, I would run through
the mountains and valleys at night.

Si j' étais un cheval, je courrais
à travers montagnes et vallées, la nuit.

Patricia, age 5.

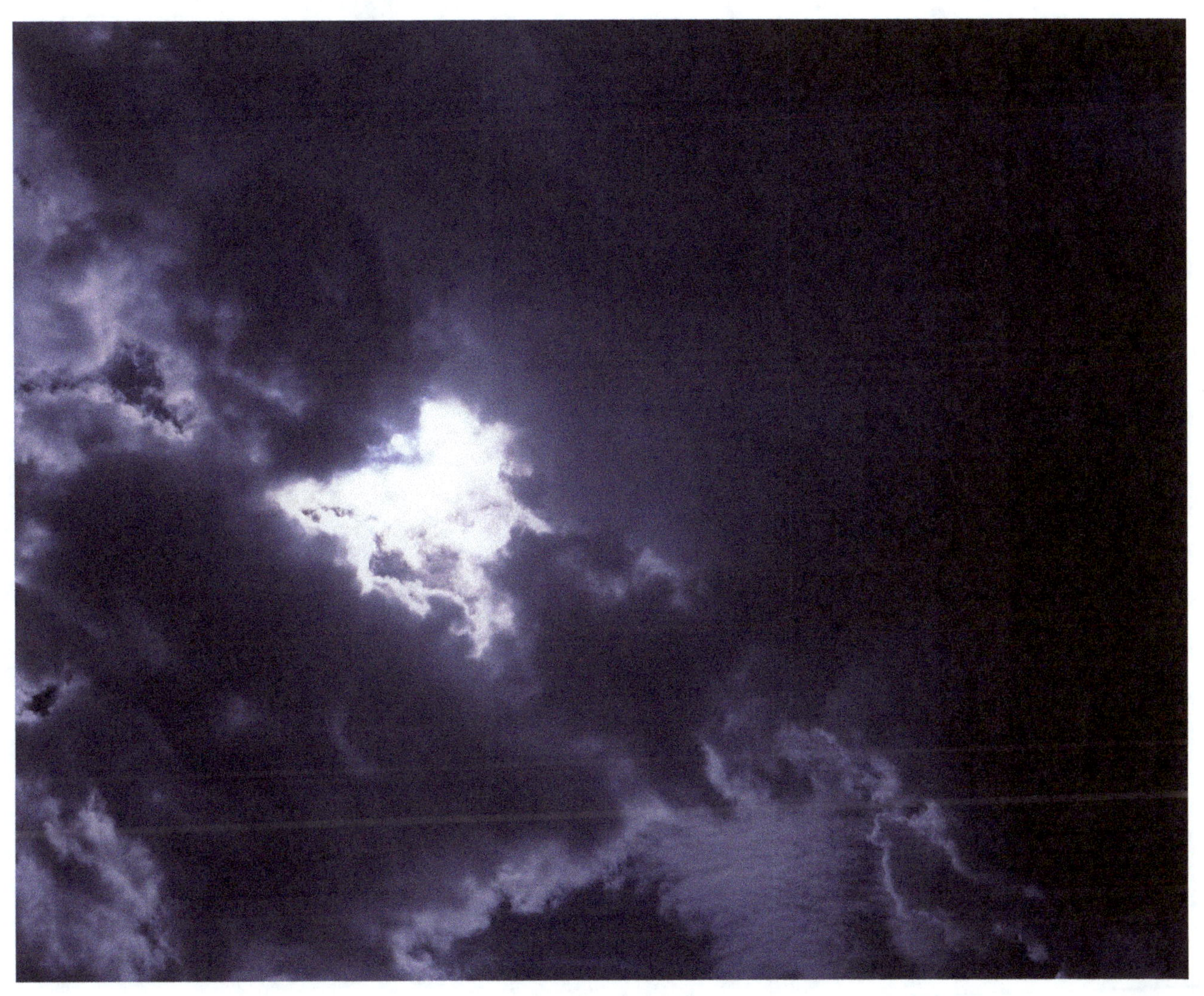

White Horse

The sun is bright, fiery
Like a burning sphere of life.

Le soleil est brillant, enflammé comme
une sphère brûlante de vie.

Brandon, age 12.

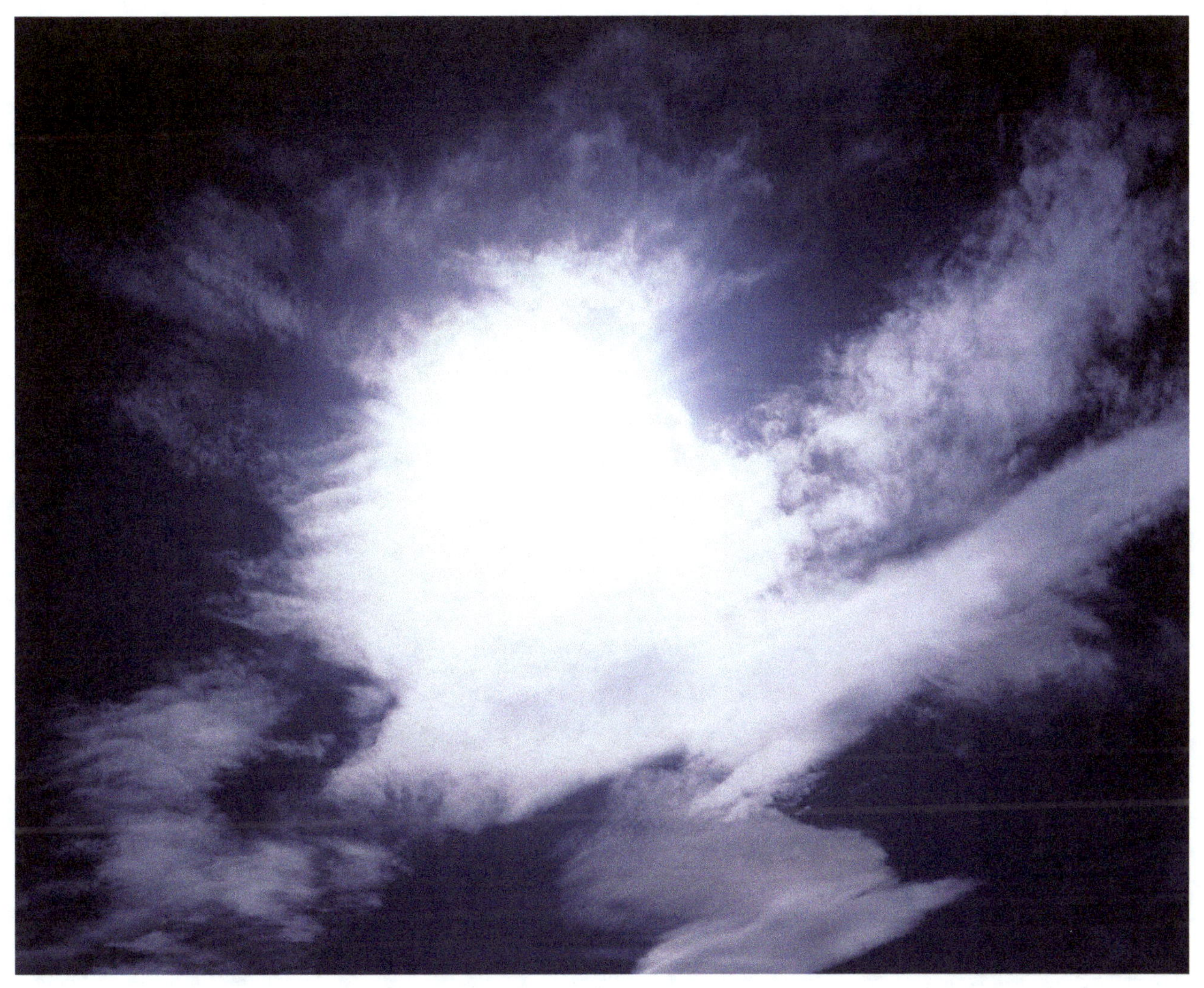

Cosmic Cloud

Angels have halos, wings, white dresses, and yellow shoes.

Les anges ont des auréoles, des ailes,
des robes blanches et des chaussures jaunes.

Stephanie, age 8.

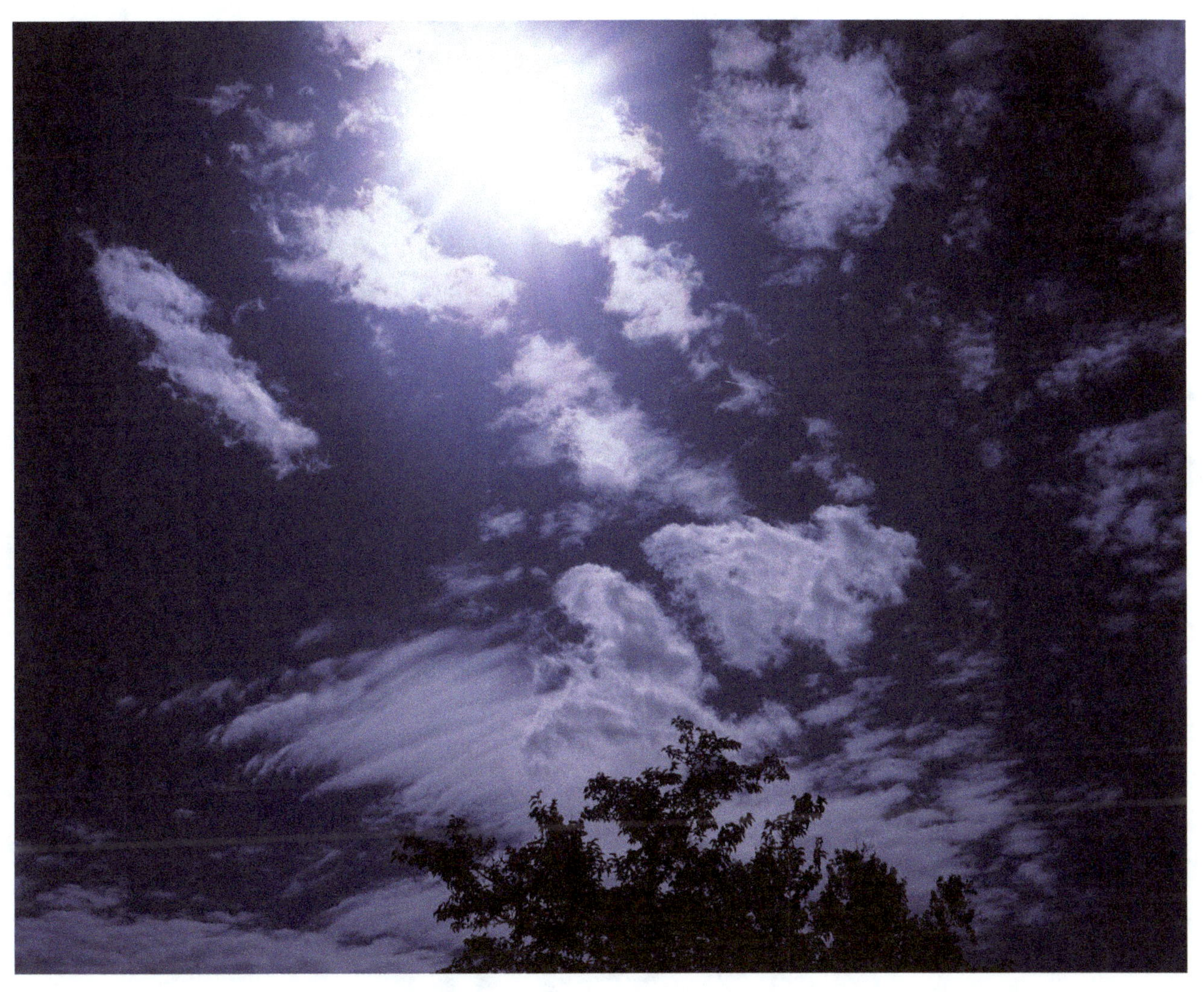

Angel Wings

Always present but never the same. Its brightness is here, while its darkness fills the night somewhere far away.

Toujours présent mais jamais pareil. Sa brillance est ici pendant que sa sombriété rempli la nuit quelque part, très loin.

Evie, age 12.

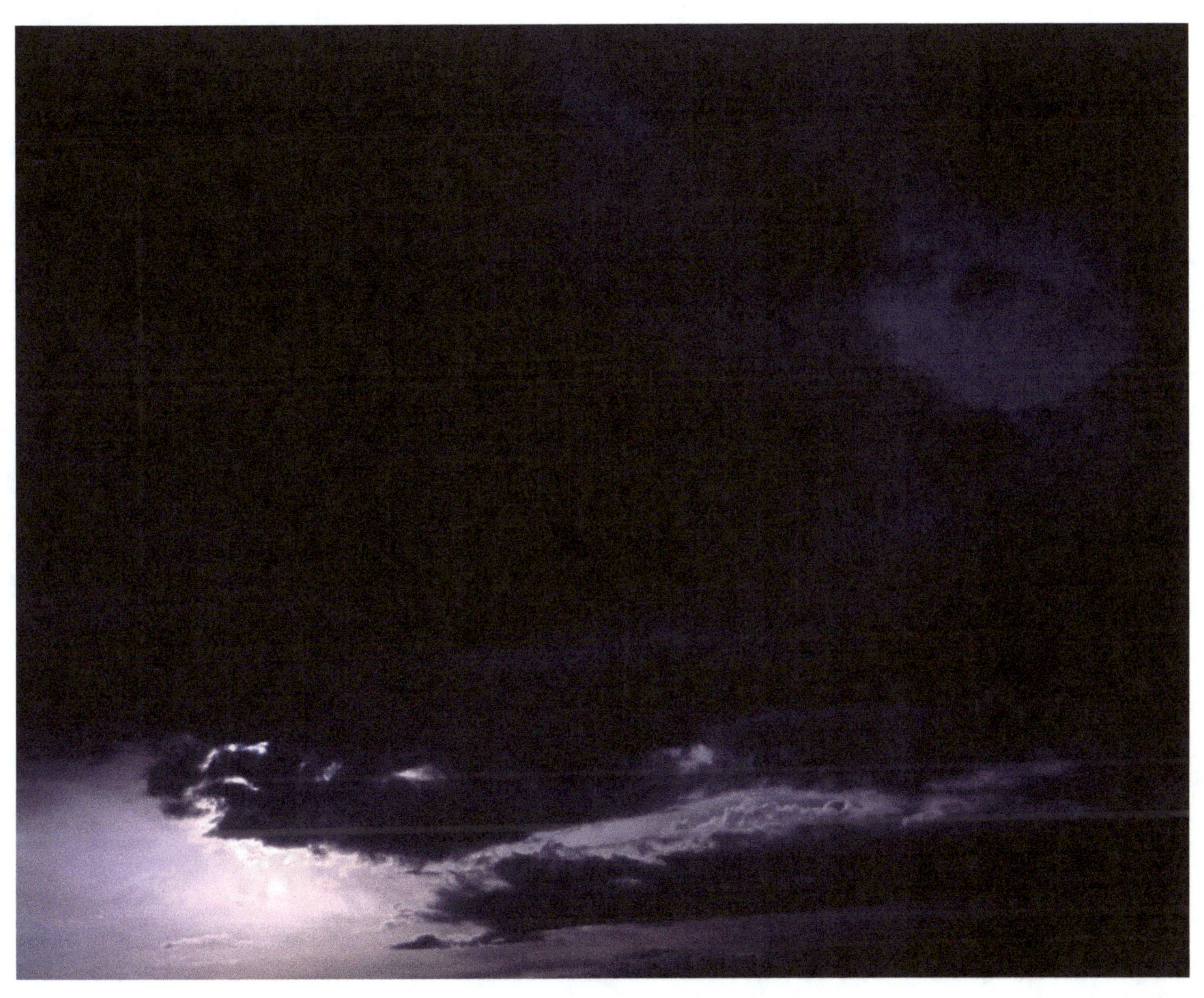

Great Everything

You know you're in love when you can't remember being as happy as you are right now.

Vous savez que vous êtes amoureux quand vous ne pouvez pas vous souvenir d'avoir jamais été aussi heureux qu' en ce moment même.

Kate, age 14.

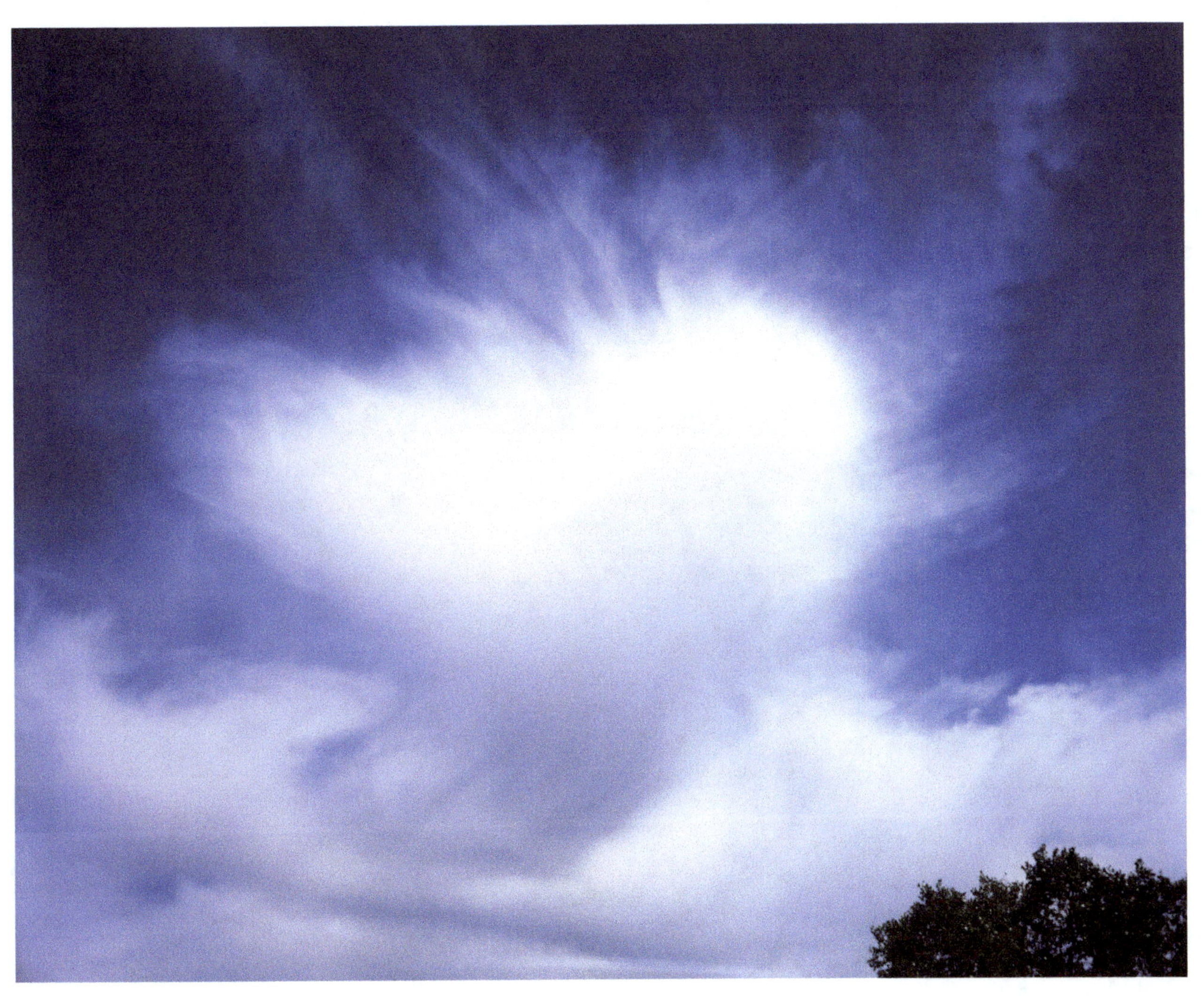

Heart Cloud

A donut tastes like sugar made from happiness.

Un beignet a le goût du sucre, fait de bonheur.

Brooke, age 16.

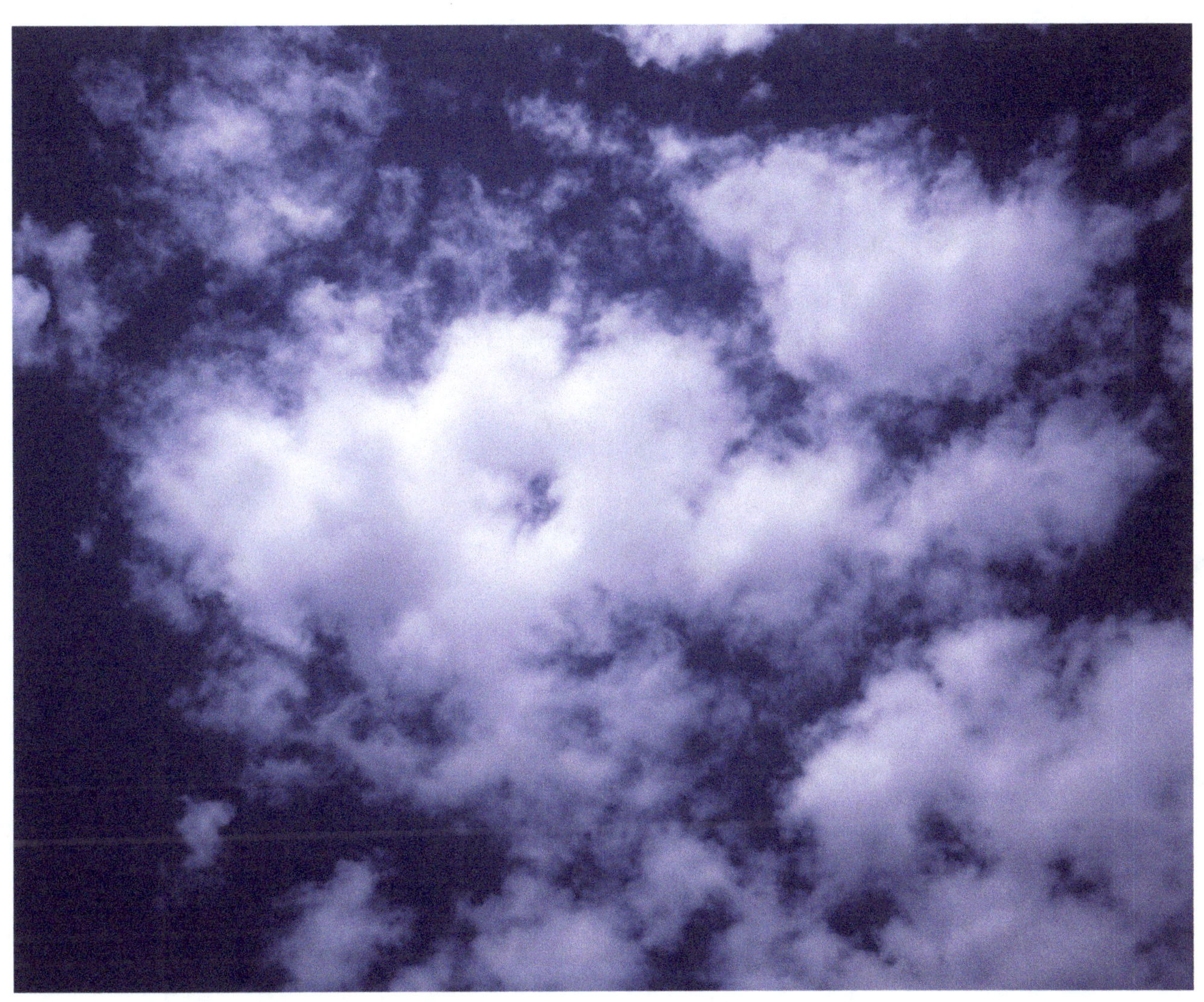

Donut Cloud

If I were a cloud, I would watch all the children playing.

Si j' étais un nuage, je regarderais les enfants au jeu.

Calin, age 6.

Child of God

Freedom is like a bird taking flight for the first time.

La liberté, c'est comme un oiseau qui prend son premier vol.

Grayson, age 15.

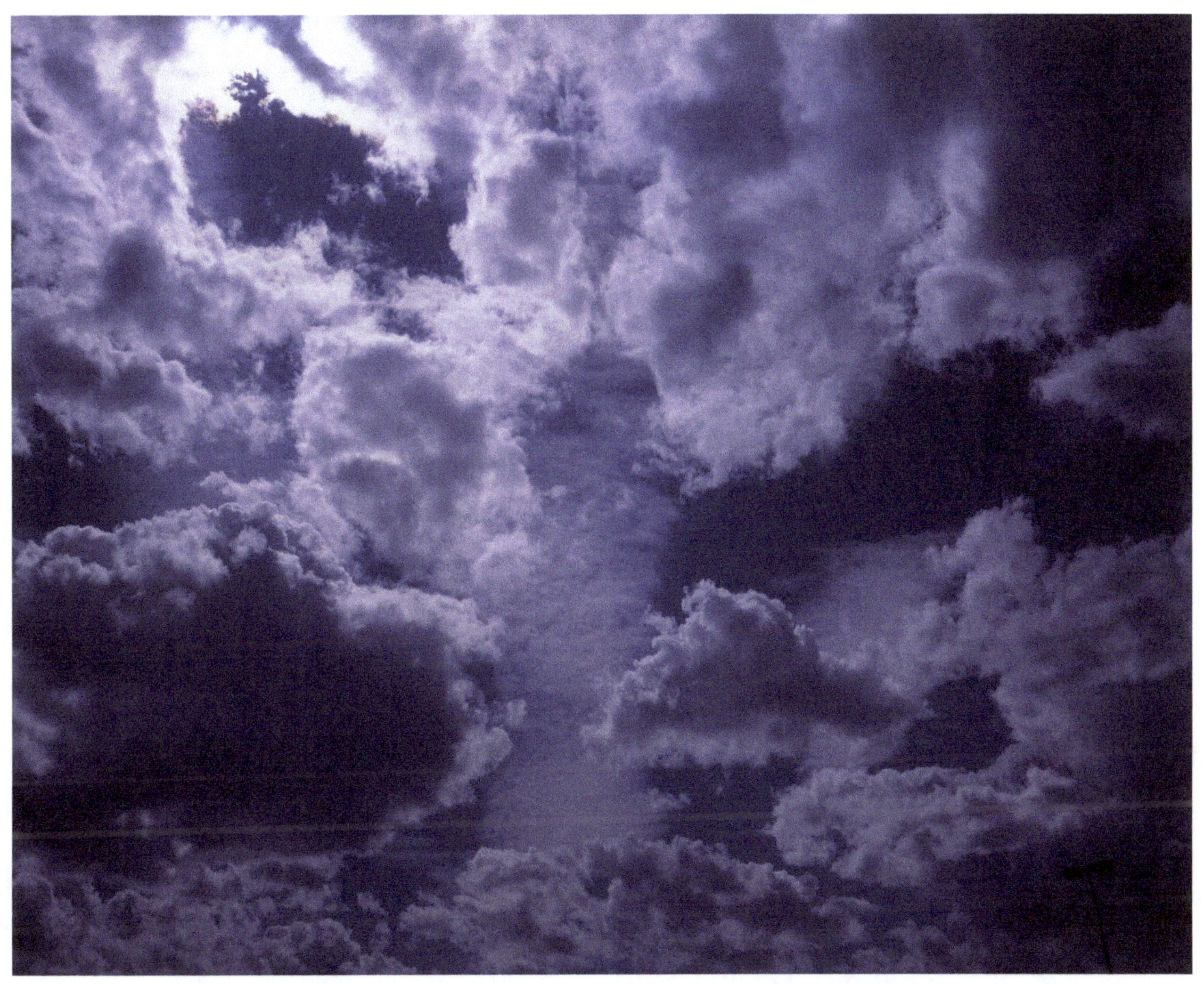

Flying

I'm as free as a ship having no destination.

Je suis aussi libre qu'un navire sans destination.

Genna, age 16.

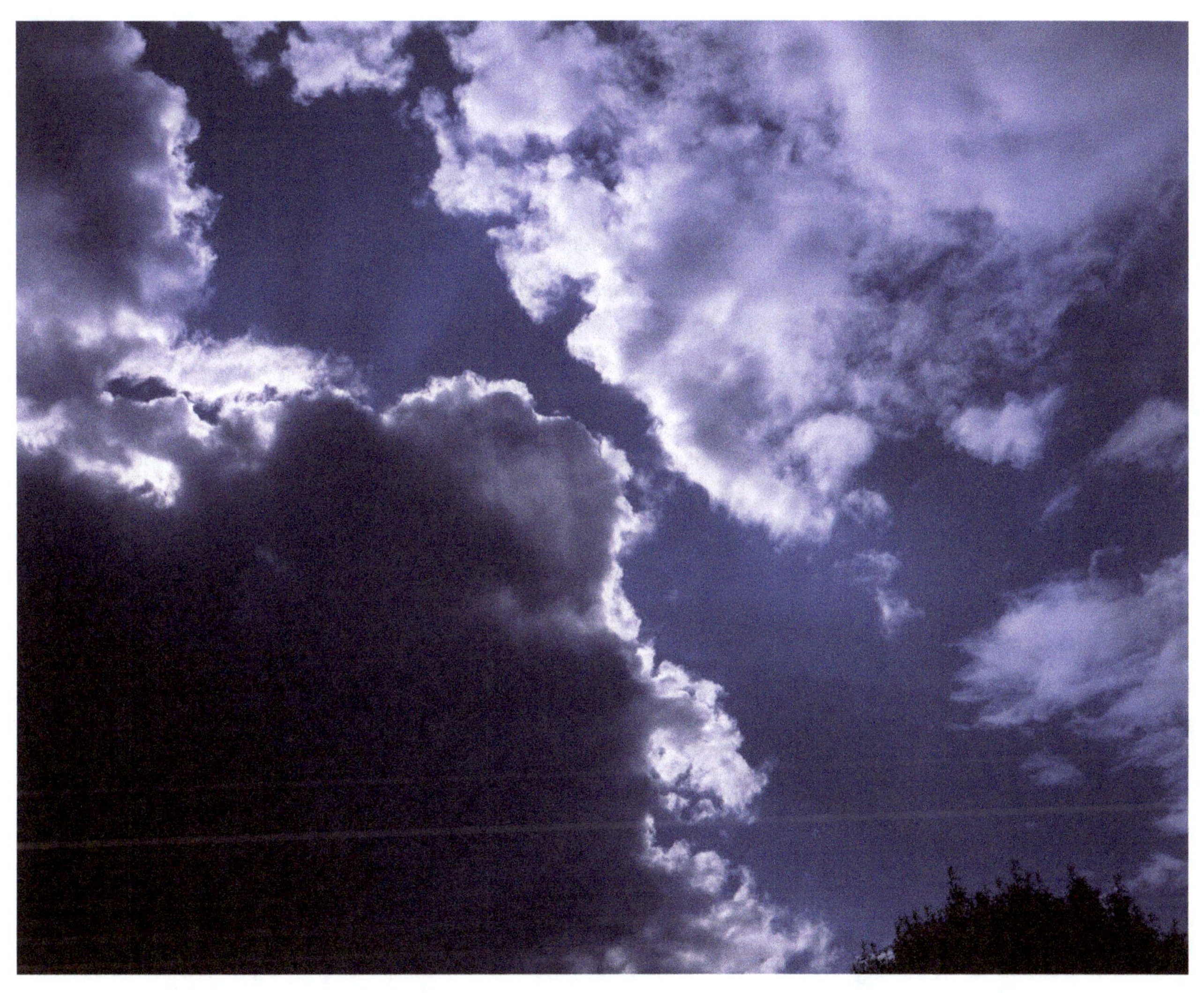

Blue Space

A storm comes and our light becomes frightened, and it hides.
The light becomes brave enough to fight back.
It is the light that brightens our storm-filled days.
Hope that a storm won't come again to frighten our light away.

Un orage arrive et effraie et il se cache.
La lumière devient courageuse, suffisamment pour se battre.
C'est la lumière qui illumine nos jours orageux.
L'espoir qu' un orage ne reviendra pas encore,
pour faire peur à notre lumière.

Kristina, age 12.

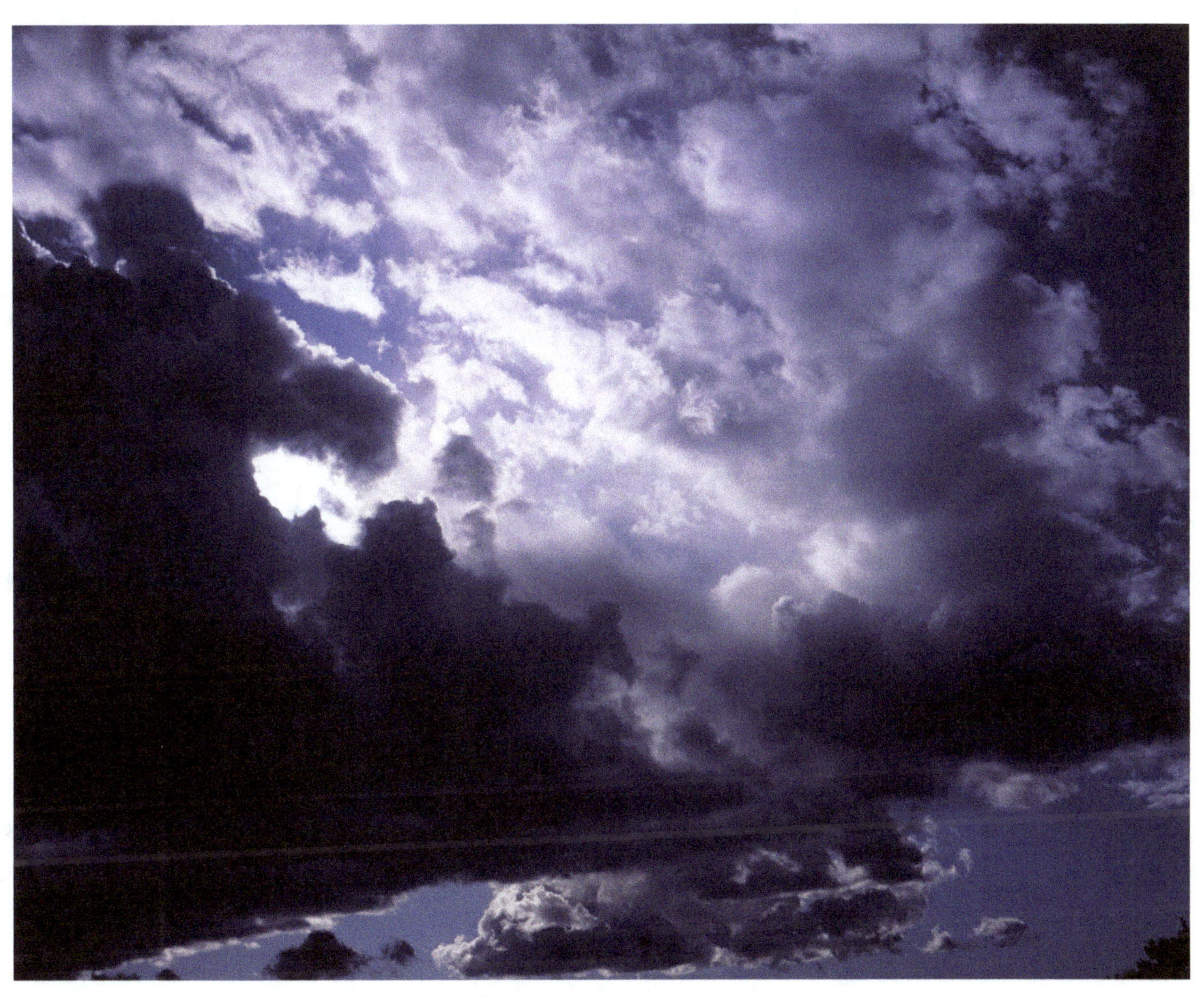

Approaching Light

Clouds sail across the sky as if it was a beautiful sea.

Des nuages naviguent à travers le ciel comme si c' était une mer magnifique.

Kyndal, age 12.

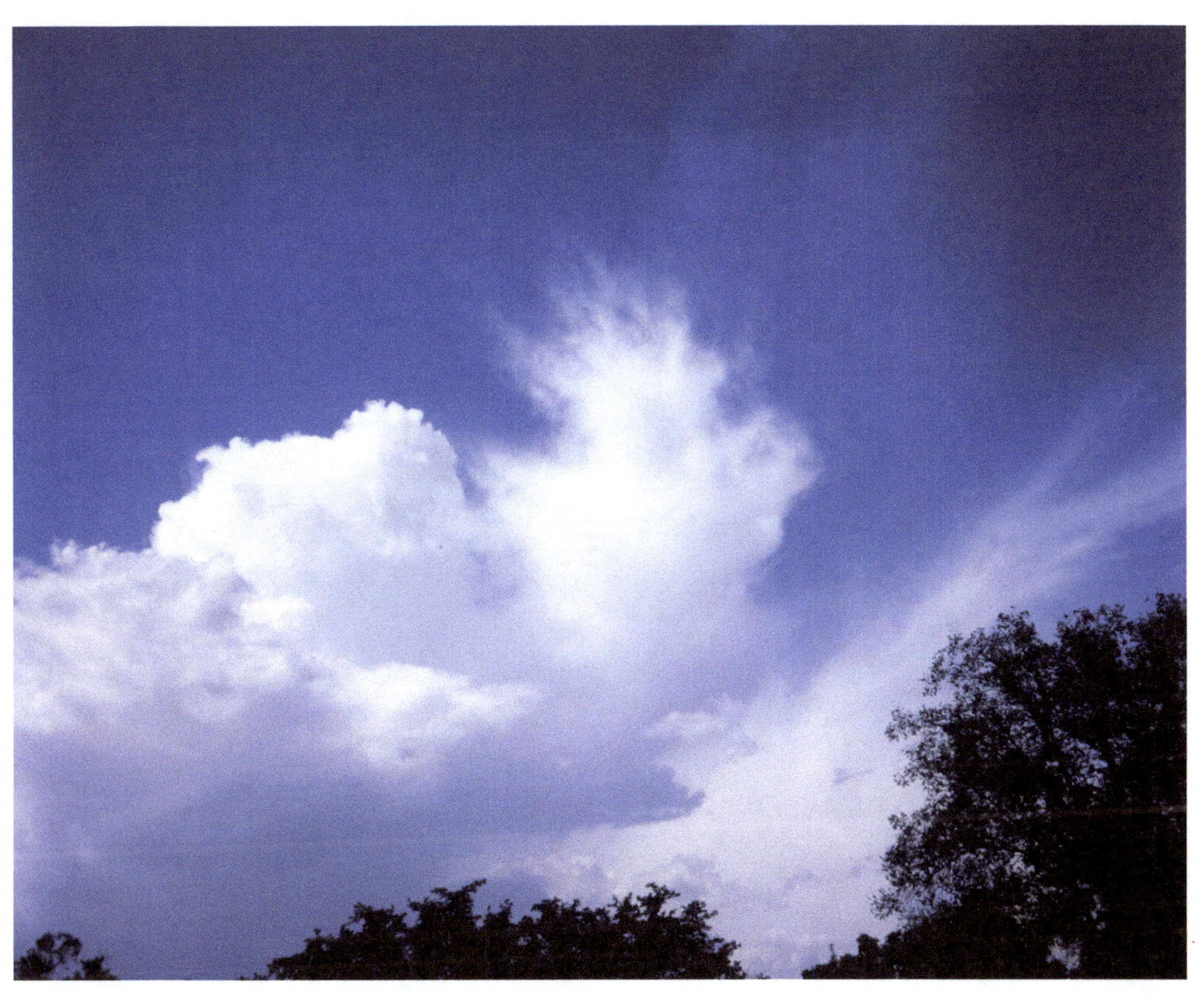

Indian Clouds

Courage is looking for life through blurry eyes and not being afraid.

Le courage, c'est de faire face à la vie avec une vision floue, sans peur.

Rachel, age 17.

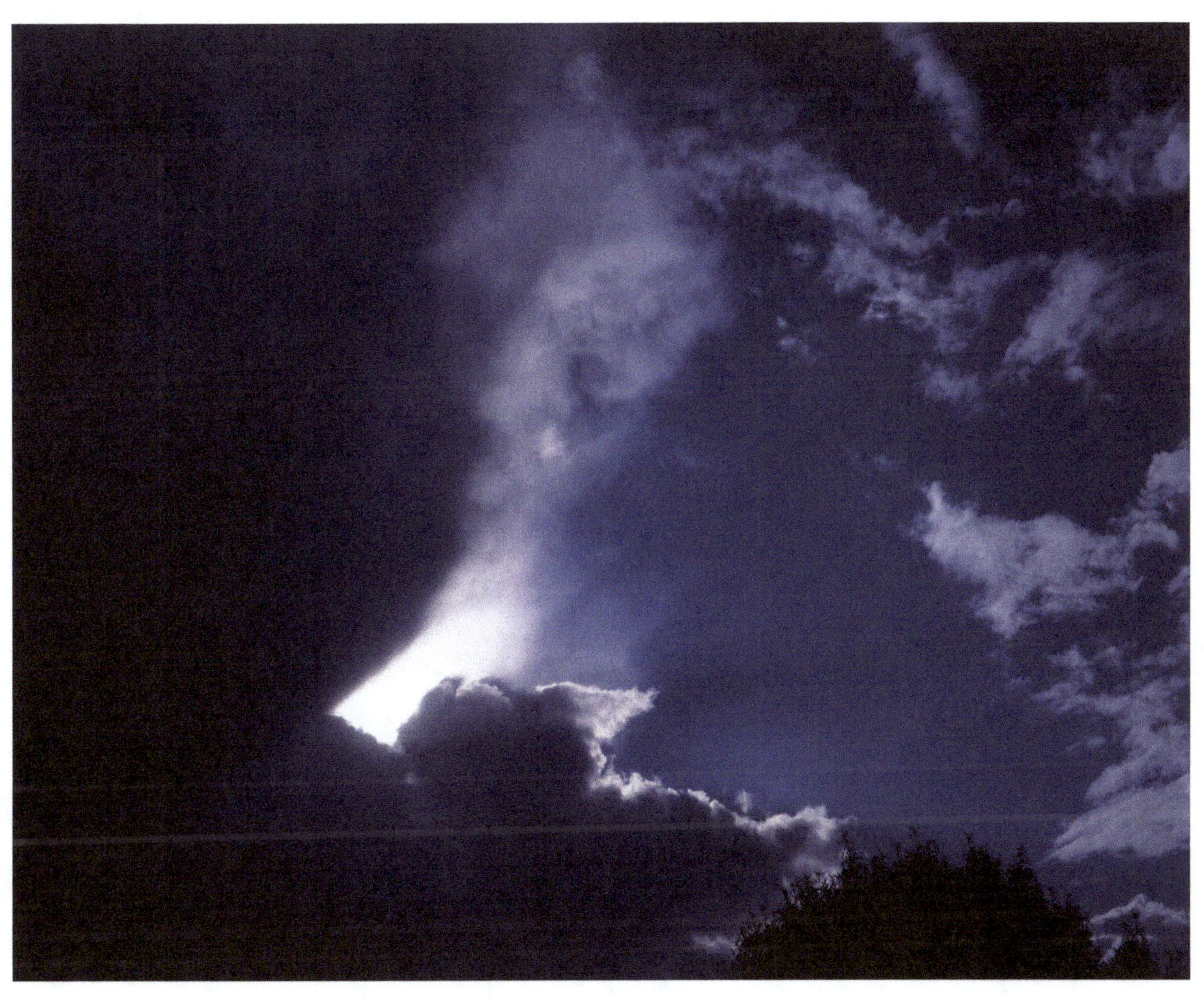

Hidden

The illuminating presence of the sky
Is what helps us stay alive.
Up above is where they float.
The sky the sea, the clouds a boat.

La présence illuminante du ciel.
Nous aide à rester vivant.
Là-haut c'est où ils flottent.
Le ciel, la mer, les nuages, un bateau.

Ben, age 12.

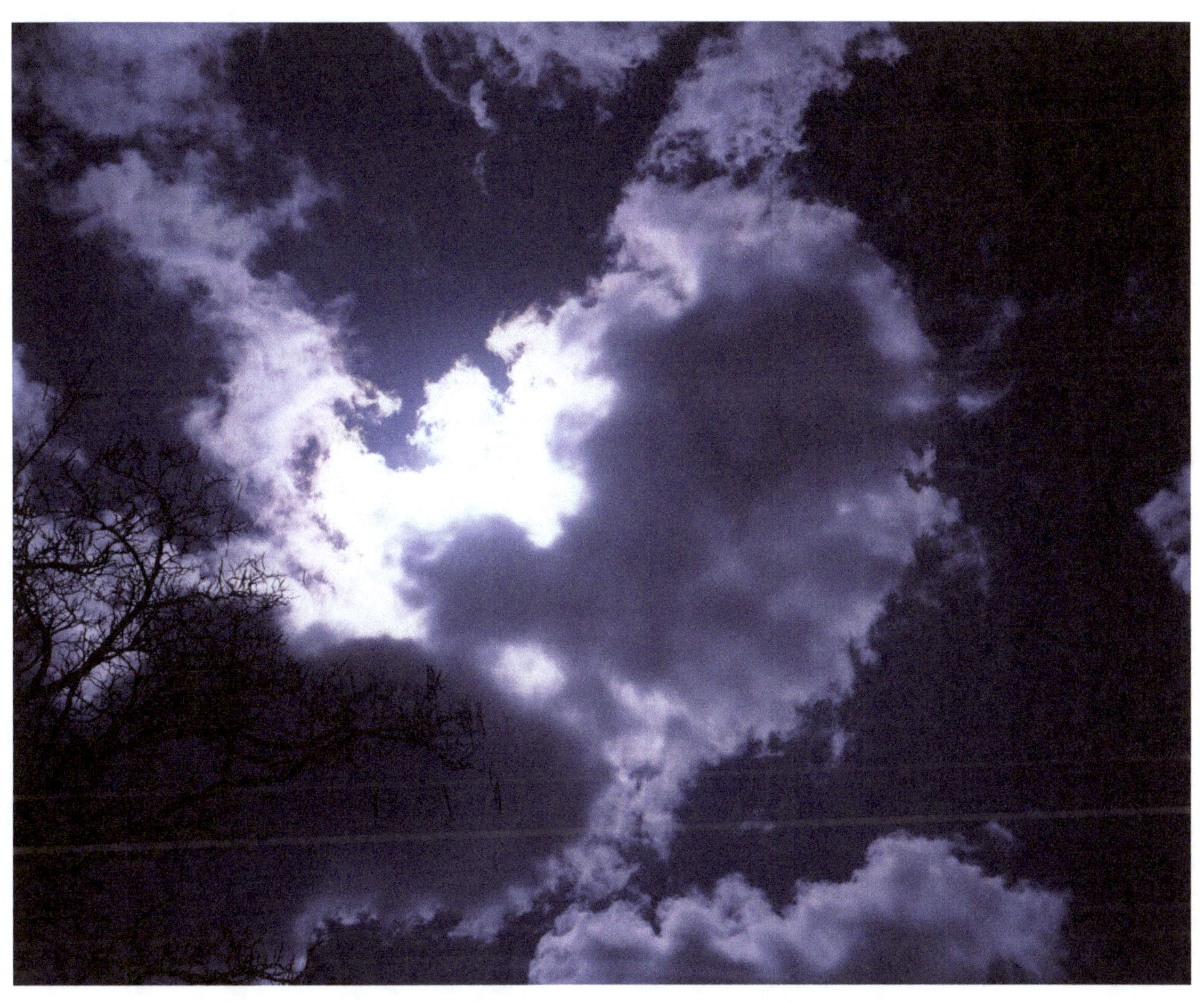

Light Creatures

Even if the world never saw your accomplishments,
your life and soul was always full of potential in my eyes.

Même si le monde n' a jamais vu vos succès,
votre vie et votre âme étaient toujours
remplies de potenciel à mes yeux.

Haley, age 15.

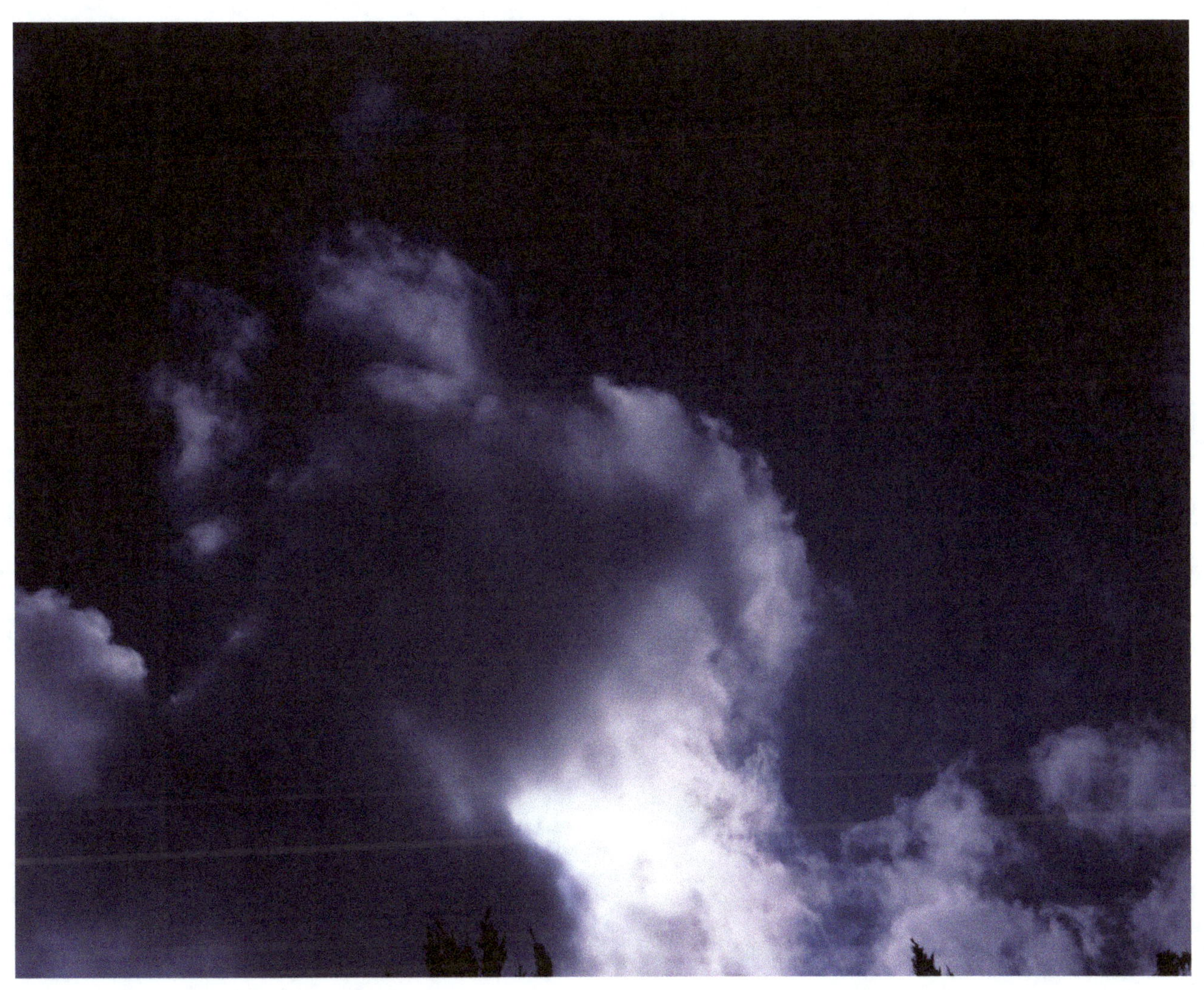

Healing Light

The sky is only a reflection of what you think of yourself.

Le ciel est la seule réflexion de ce que vous pensez de vous-même.

Regan, age 12.

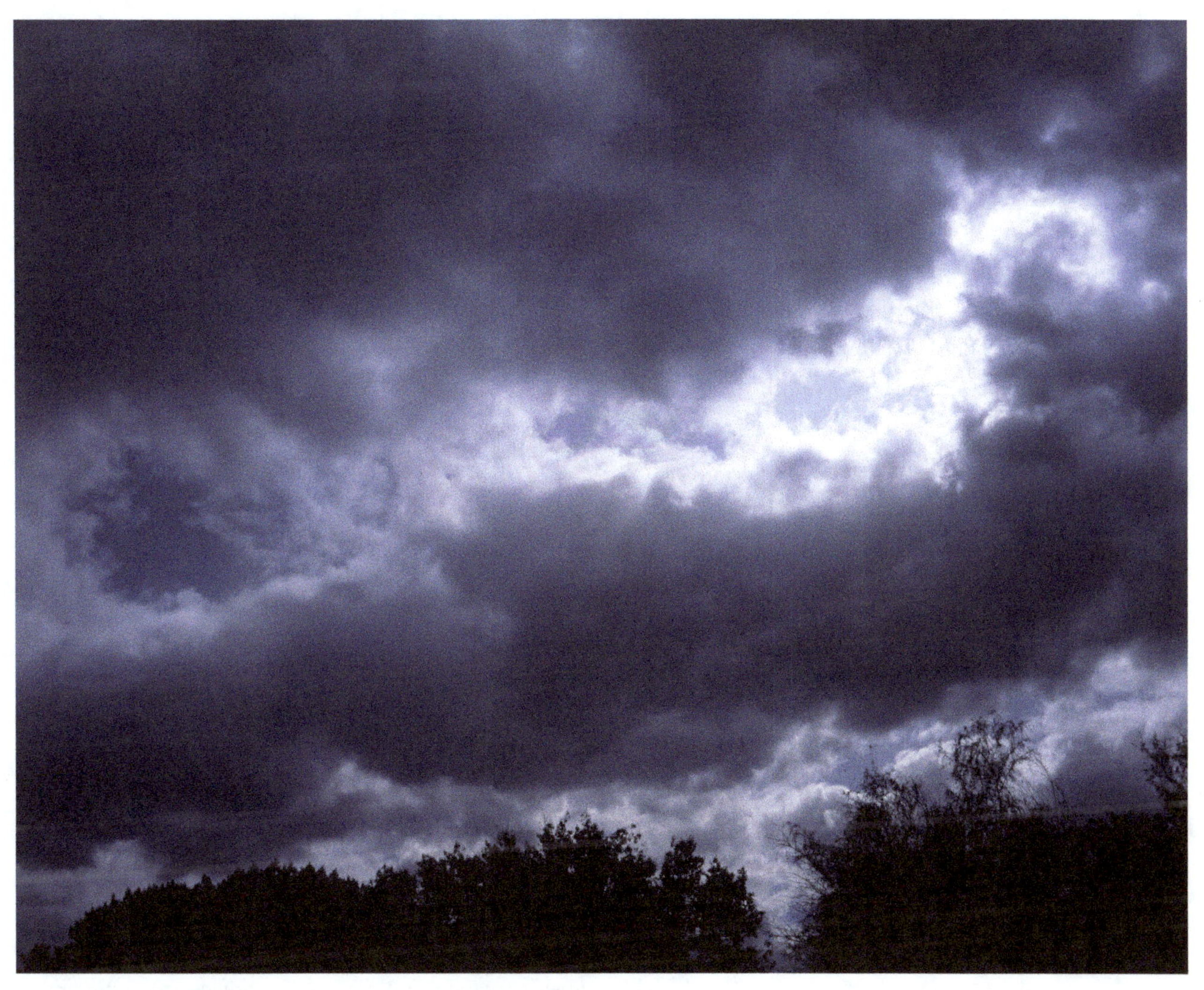

Holes in Sky

I am a boy with turquoise eyes that loves to read.
I wonder if man will ever fly.
I hear a dog popping bubbles.
I see a floating computer.
I want global warming to stop.
I am a boy with turquoise eyes that loves to read.
I pretend I'm bowling.
I feel like a bouncing koala bear.
I touch a flying octopus.
I worry about some animals that are going extinct.
I cry about diabetes.
I am a boy with turquoise eyes that loves to read.
I understand that I am 11 years old.
I say music is helpful.
I dream about trolley cars driving off their tracks
with giant chess pieces on top of them.
I try to finish my homework.
I hope for a cure to diabetes.
I am a boy with turquoise eyes that loves to read.

Je suis un gargon aux yeux turquoises, qui aime lire.
Je me demande si l'homme volera jamais.
J'entends un chien qui fait éclater des bulles.
Je vois un ordinateur qui flotte.
Je veux que le réchauffement de la planète s'arrête.
Je suis un gargon aux yeux turquoises, qui aime lire.
Je fais semblant de jouer au bowling.
Je me sens comme un koala qui saute.
Je touche un octopode qui vole.
Je me fais du souci à propos de la disparition de certains animaux.
Je pleure à propos du diabète.
Je suis un gargon aux yeux turquoises, qui aime lire.
Je comprends que j'ai onze ans.
Je dis que la musique aide.
Je rêve de tramways roulant en dehors des rails
avec des pions d'échèque géants, sur le toit.
J'essaie de finir mes devoirs.
J'espère qu'on trouvera une cure pour le diabète.
Je suis un gargon aux yeux turquoises, qui aime lire.

Theron, age 11.

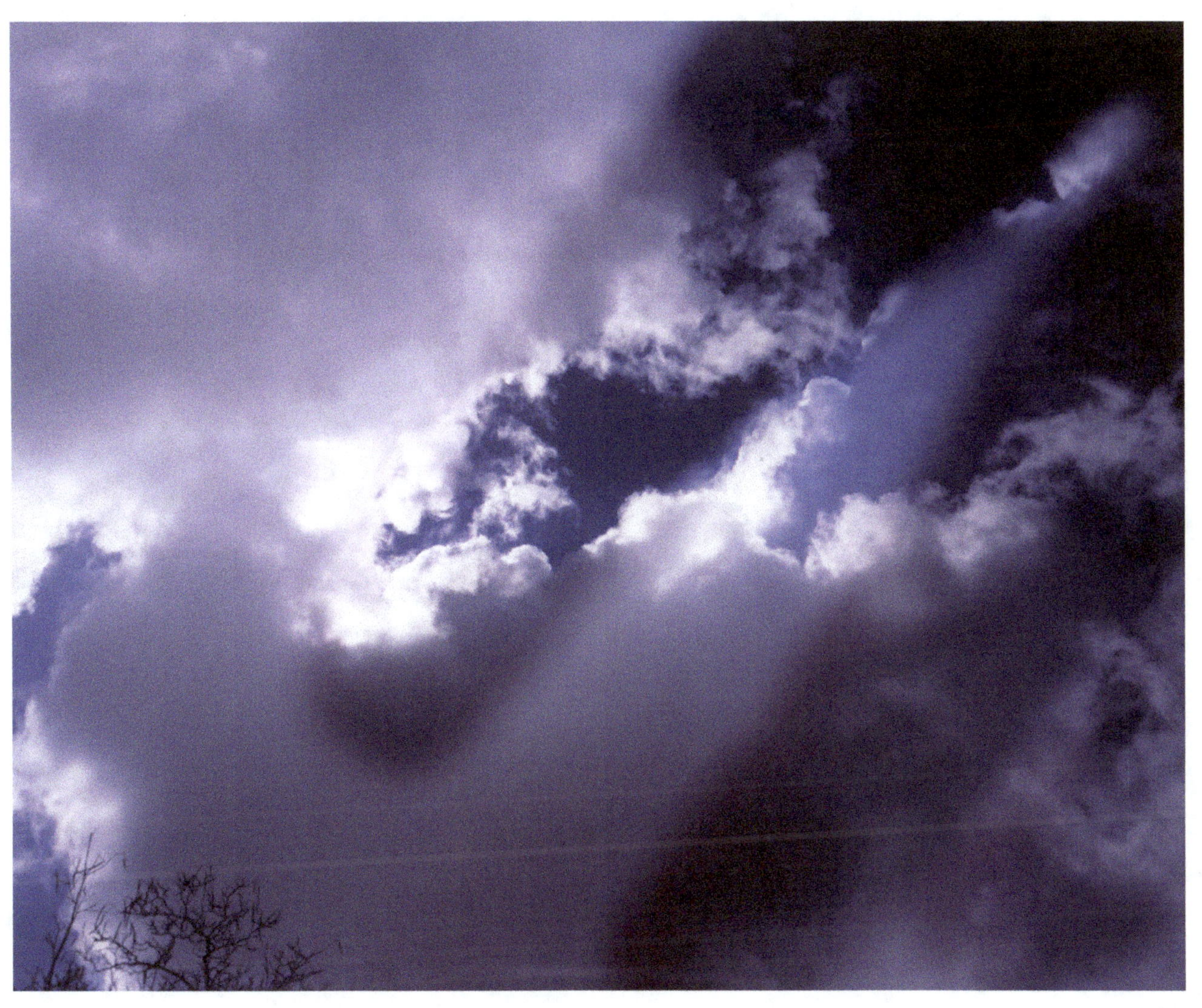

Indigo Child

Freedom is like a shooting star roaming across the night sky.

La liberté est comme une étoile filante se baladant à travers le ciel, la nuit.

Vickie, age 15.

Sky Spirit

Courage is thinking you can't do it but knowing that you can always try.

Le courage c'est de penser que vous ne pouvez pas le faire mais de savoir que vous pouvez toujours essayer.

Heather, age 15.

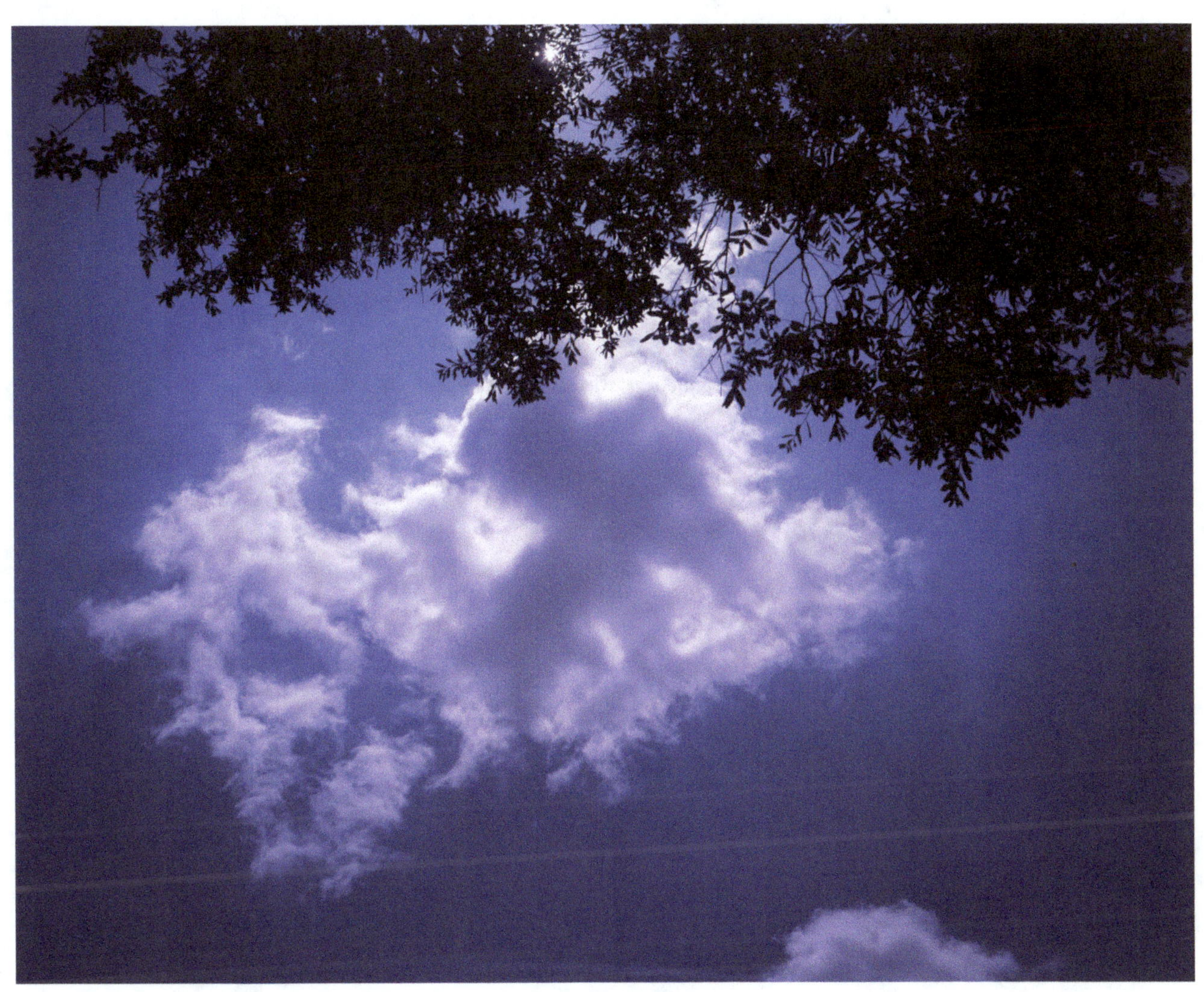

The Faithful

Every corner of the sky holds
a thousand angels watching over us.

Dans chaque coin du ciel, il y a mille anges qui nous protègent.

Lindsey, age 16.

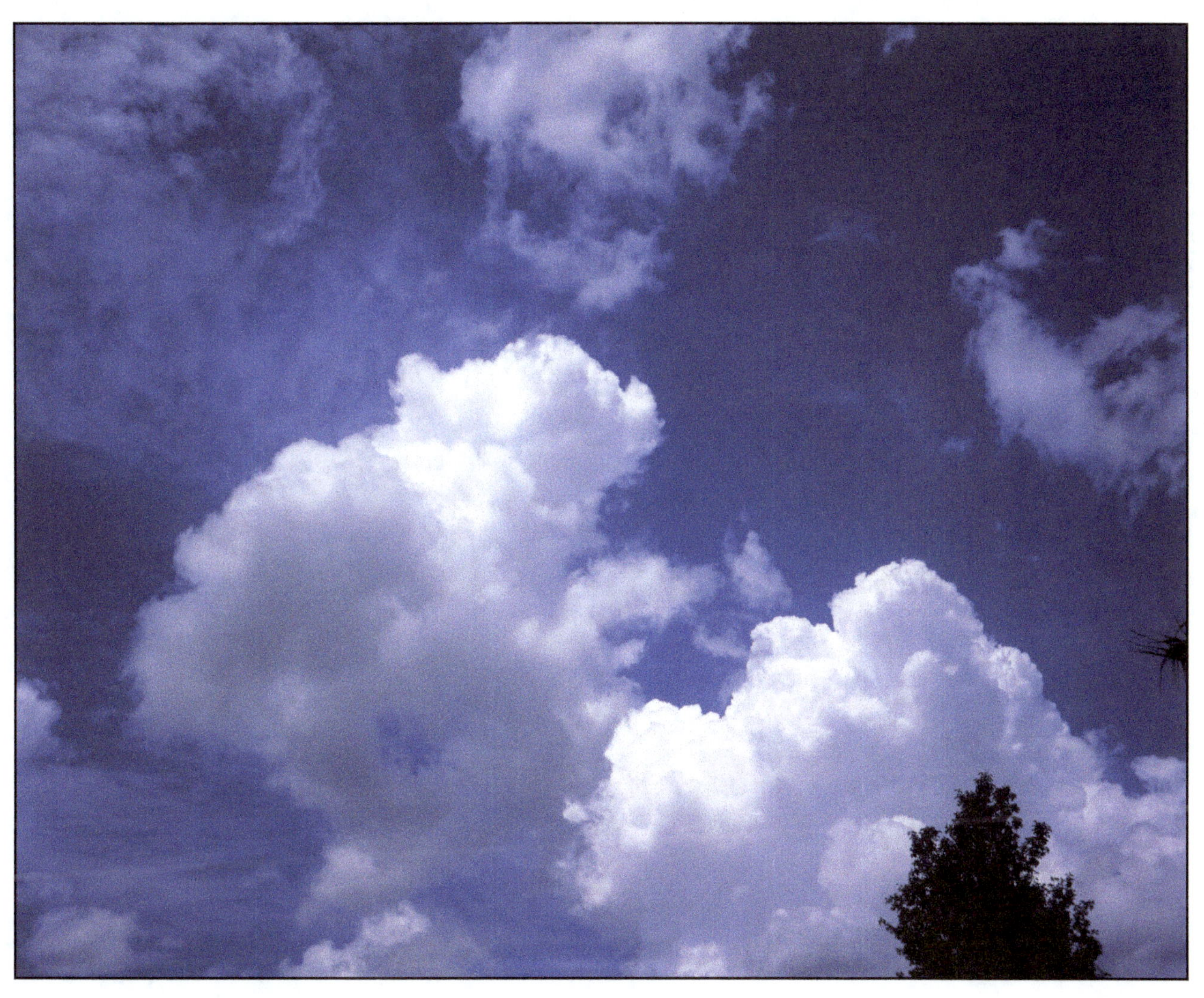

The Watchers

Like a sunrise, this awareness rises within you,
freeing you from all fear,
opening up a new passage to your life.
This marks the beginning of love and the end to life before.

Comme l'aube, cet éveillement s'élève en vous,
vous libérant de toute peur,
ouvrant un nouveau passage pour votre vie.
Ceci marque le début de l'amour et la fin de la vie précédente.

Jessica, age 17.

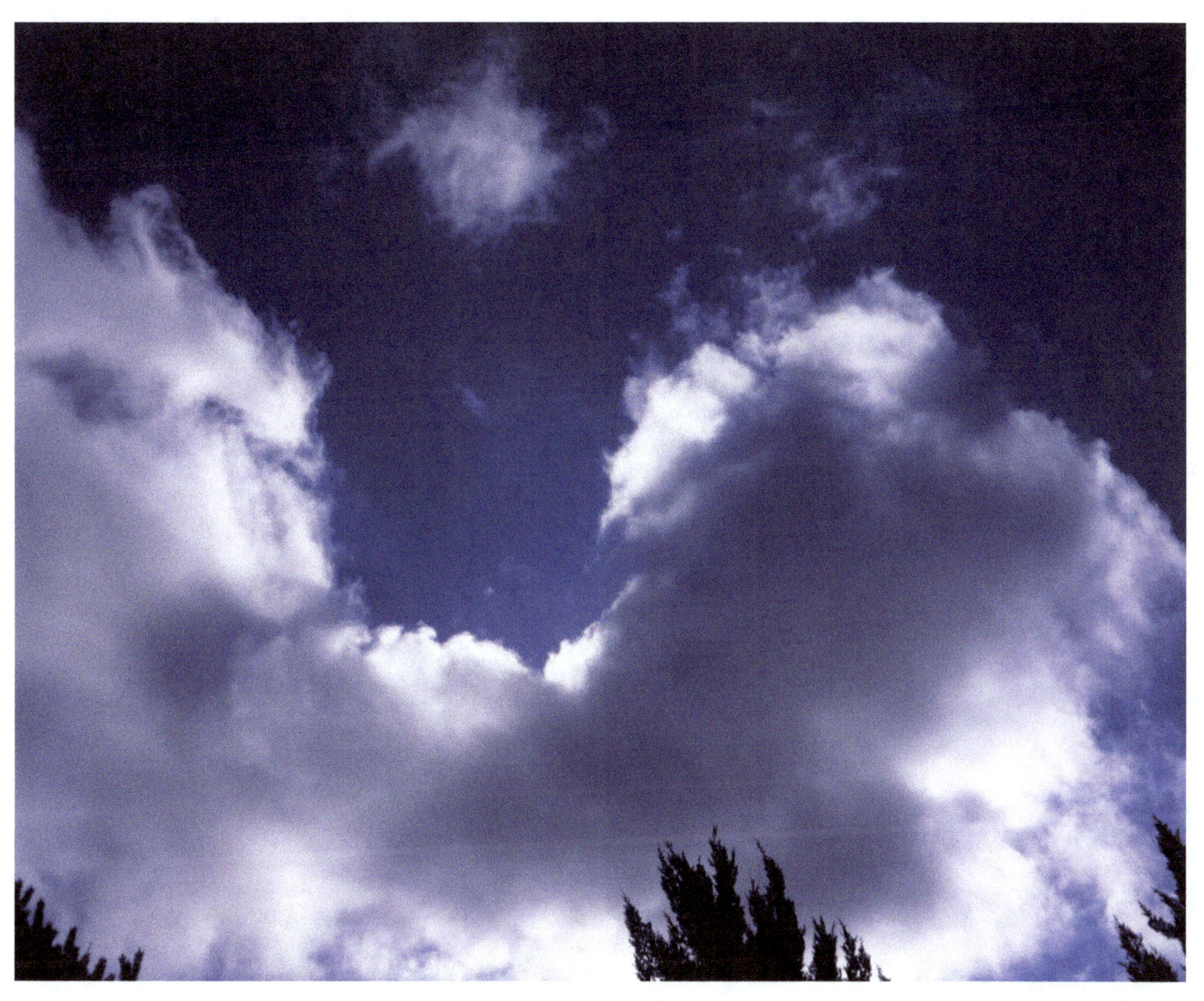

Wheel of Life

The sky is a game of wonderful creation.

Le ciel est un jeu de création merveilleuse.

Natalie, age 12.

Holy Event

Windy Clouds
cotton balls on a string
pulled by time, pushed by wind
float overhead
held in the sky by the push of wind.

Nuages balayés par le vent,
boules de coton sur un fil,
tirés par le temps, poussés par le vent et
qui flottent au-dessus de la tête
tenus dans le ciel par le vent qui pousse.

Forge, age 12.

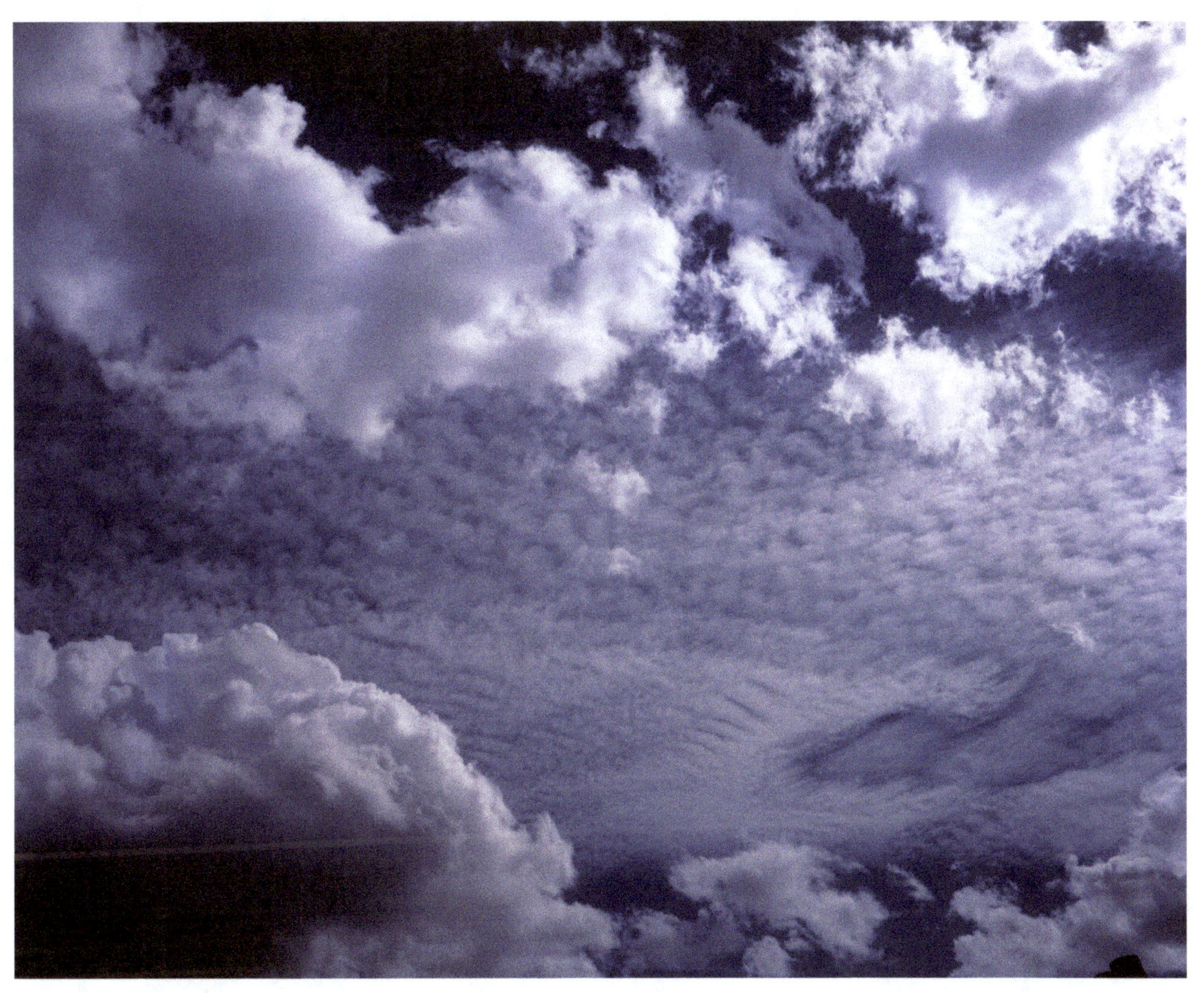

Sky Fish

Life changes with the circumstances, but love remains the same.

La vie change avec les circonstances, mais l'amour reste le même.

Rachel, age 16.

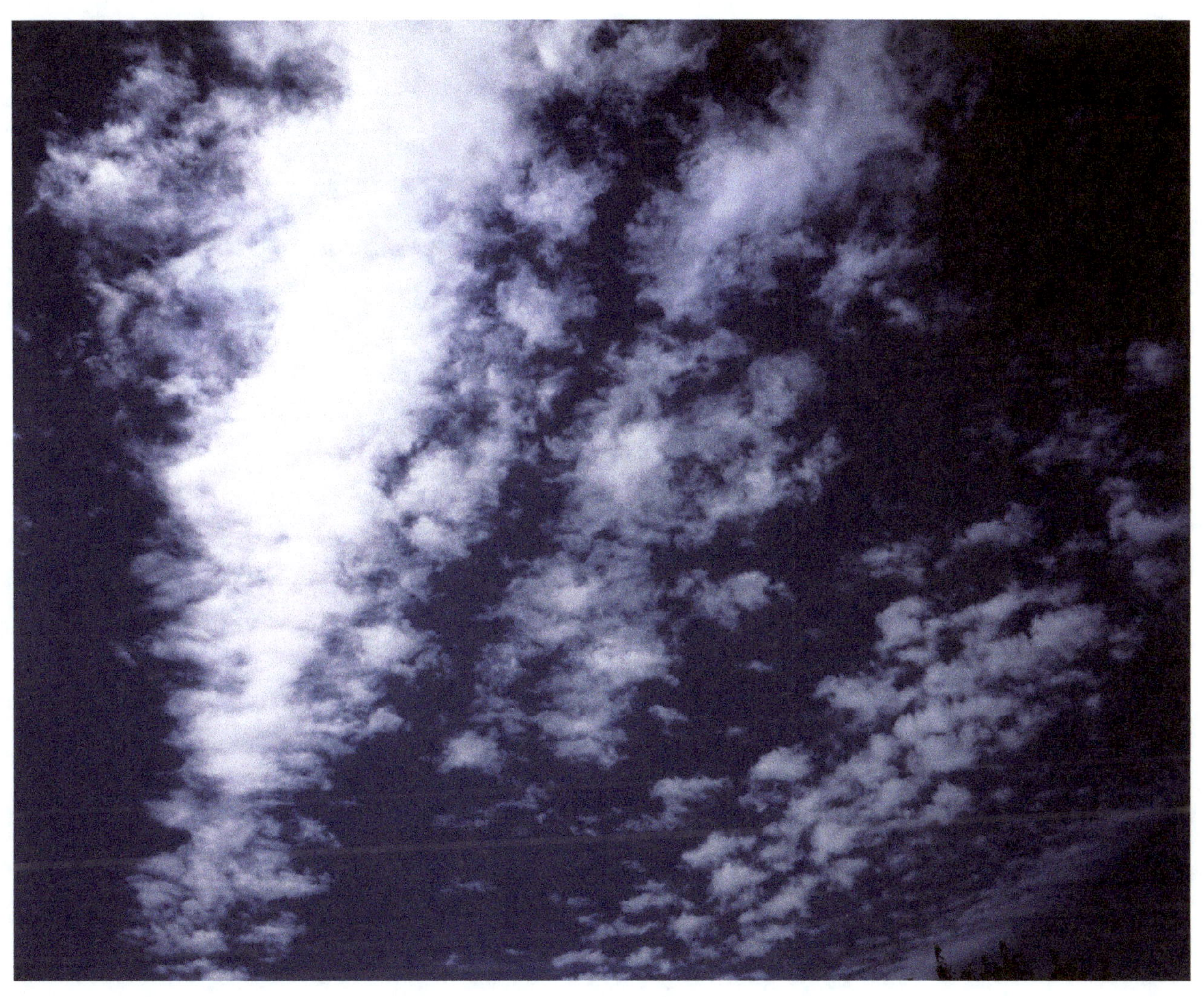

Vortex

Happiness is when you feel like taking a rocket to the moon and dancing among the stars.

Le bonheur c'est quand vous avez envie de prendre une fusée vers la lune et de danser parmi les étoiles.

Kristy Katherine, age 15.

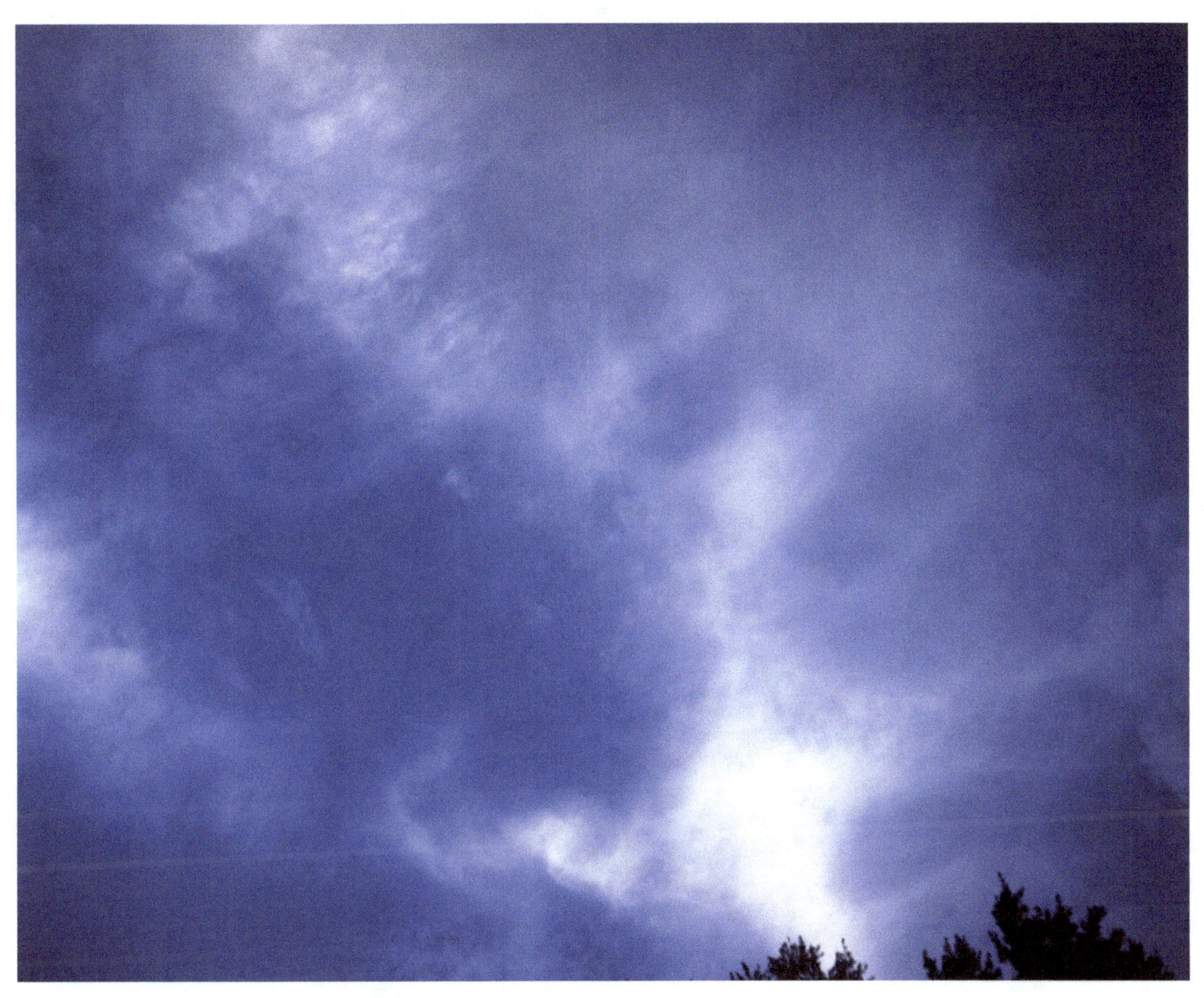

Light Dancers

You can't define love,
because that would take away all the magic in the world.

Vous ne pouvez pas déterminer l'amour,
parce que cela enlèverait toute la magie du monde.

Savannah, age 16.

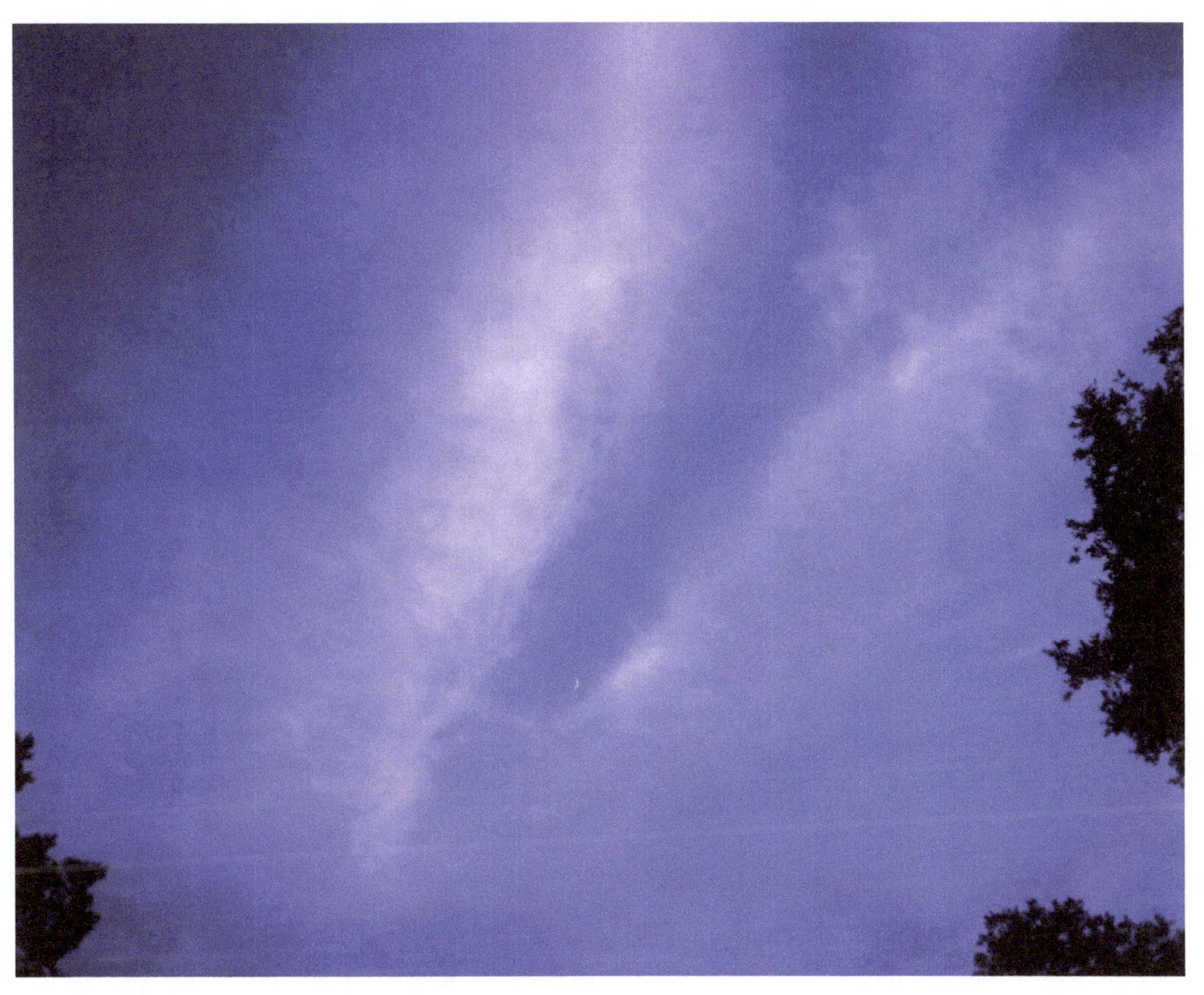

Mystic Moon

Happiness is setting your alarm clock at 2:00 a.m.
so that it feels like a Saturday morning
when you have 4 more hours 'til you have to get up.

Le bonheur c'est de mettre la sonnerie du réveil à deux heures
du matin et on dirait que c'est samedi matin et
que vous avez encore quatre heures avant de vous lever du lit.

Maggie, age 16.

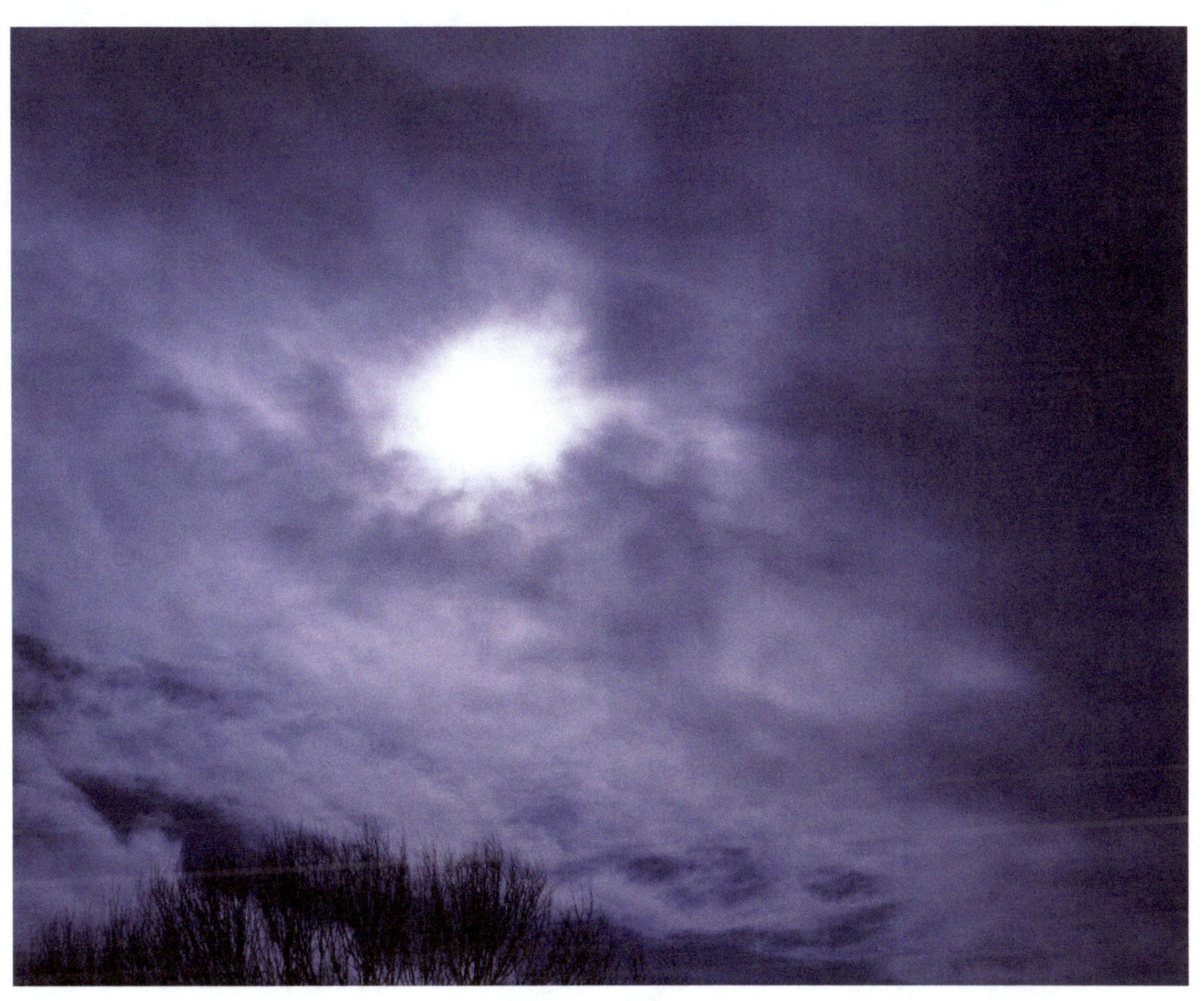

Portal

Peace of mind is one of the most precious gifts we can receive.

La tranquilité d'esprit est un des plus précieux cadeaux que nous pouvons recevoir.

Lindy, age 15.

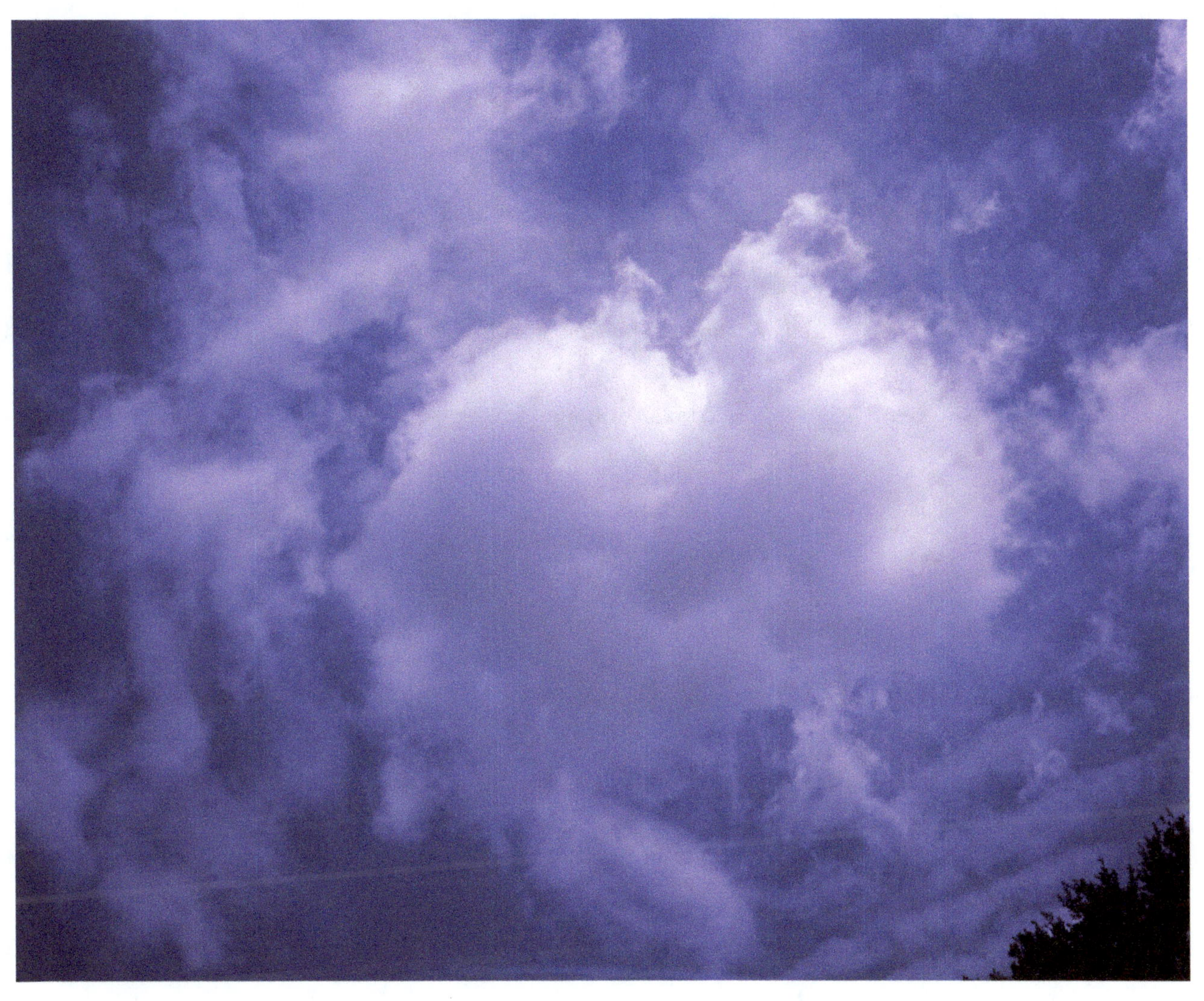

Renewal

Happiness is finding your destiny.

Le bonheur, c'est de trouver votre destiné.

Alexandra, age 15.

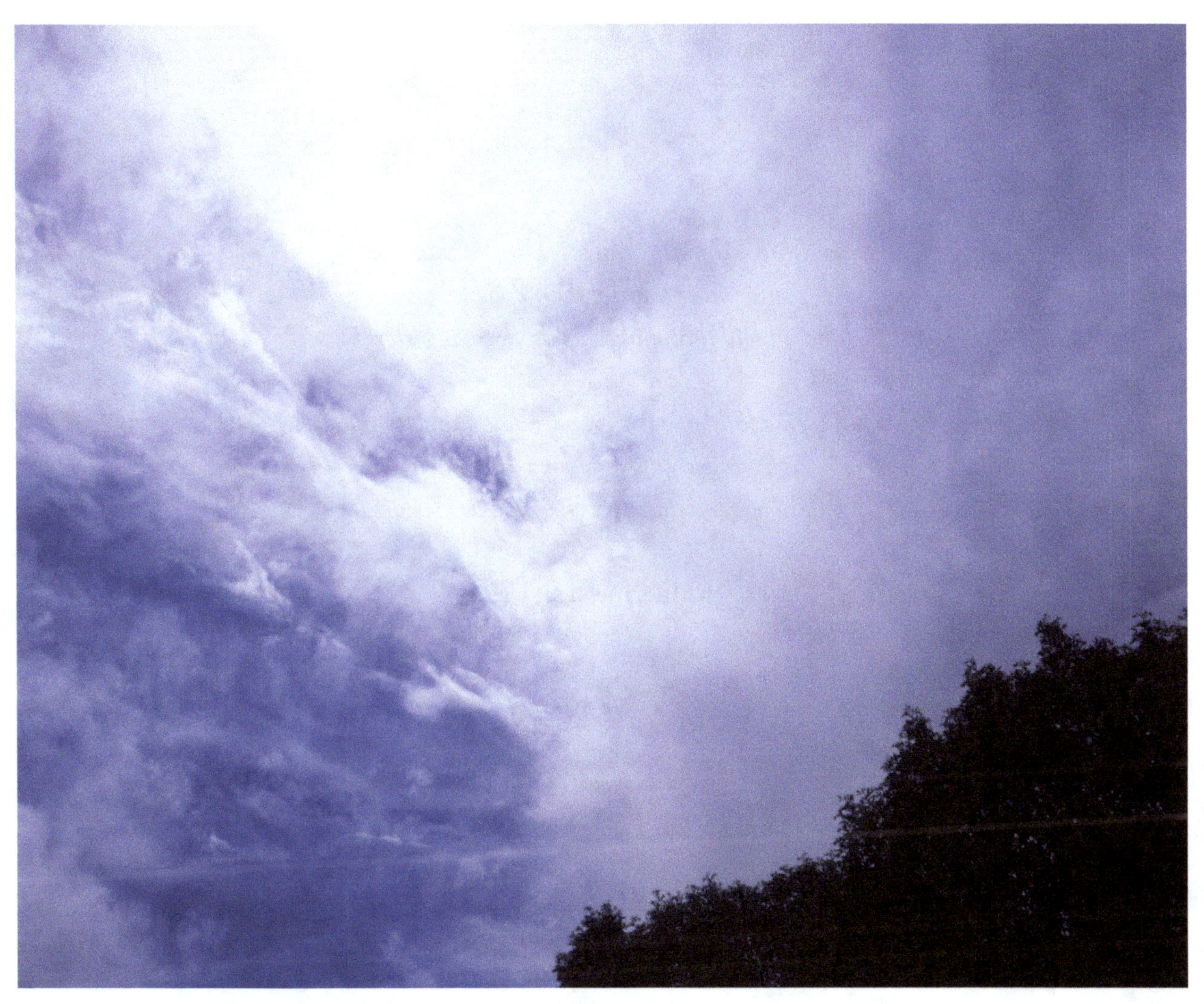

Sacred Father

Friendship, stronger than steel, softer than clouds,
more faithful than dogs,
and a bond that makes us as close as sisters.

L'amitié, plus forte que l'acier, plus douce que les nuages,
plus fidèle que les chiens, et un lien
qui nous rend aussi proches que des soeurs.

Katherine, age 17.

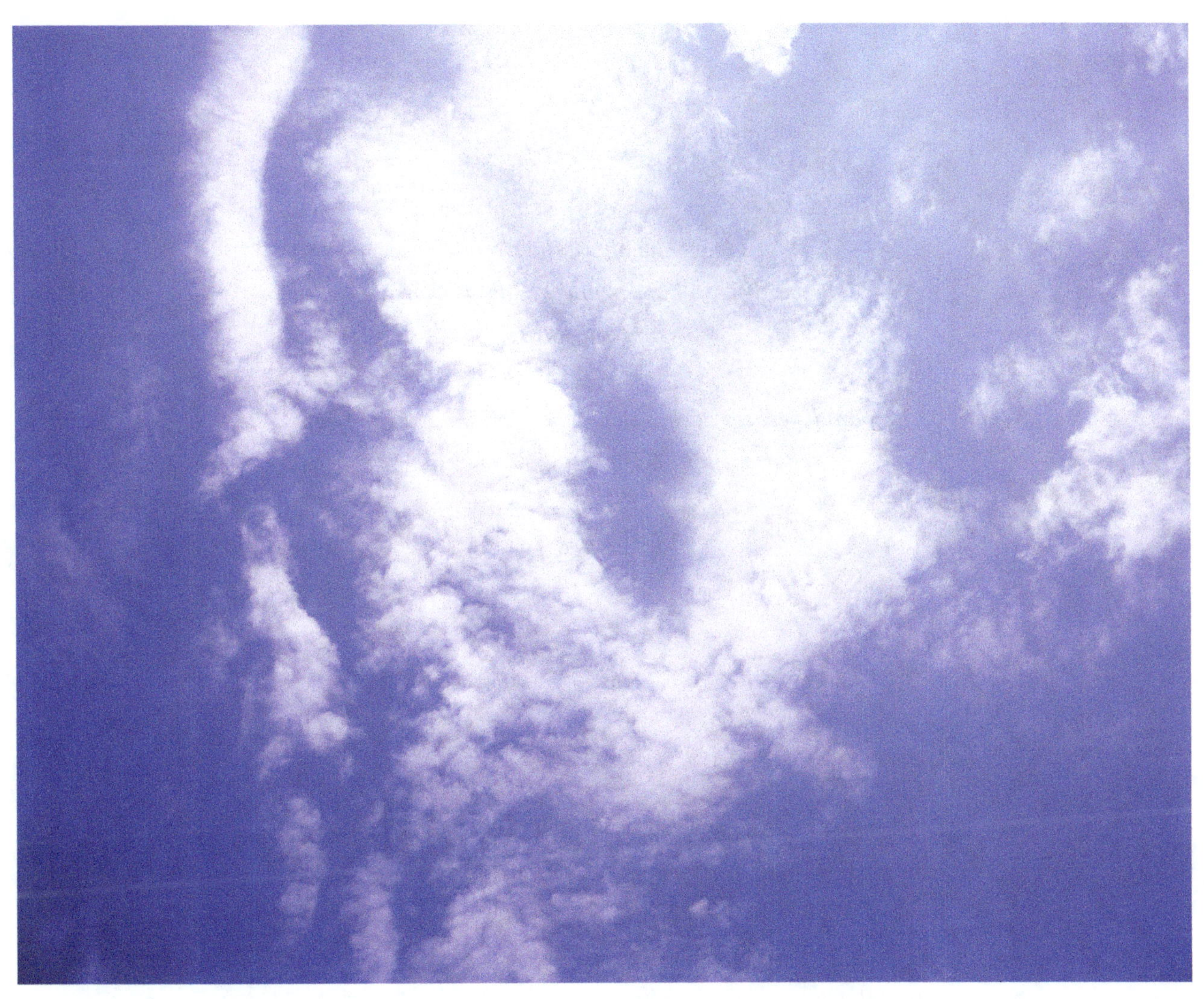

Sacred Mother

Heaven is above the clouds
and there's houses and buildings there
— and our kitties.

Le paradis est au-dessus des nuages et il y a des maisons
et des bâtiments, là, et nos chats.

·

Molly, age 7.

Safe

Mystery is like an igloo with water lilies growing wild.

Le mytère, c'est comme un igloo avec des nénuphars qui poussent sauvagement.

Lilly, age 15.

Star Child

Happiness is falling asleep on the beach.

Le bonheur, c'est de s'endormir sur la plage.

Ashlyn, age 17.

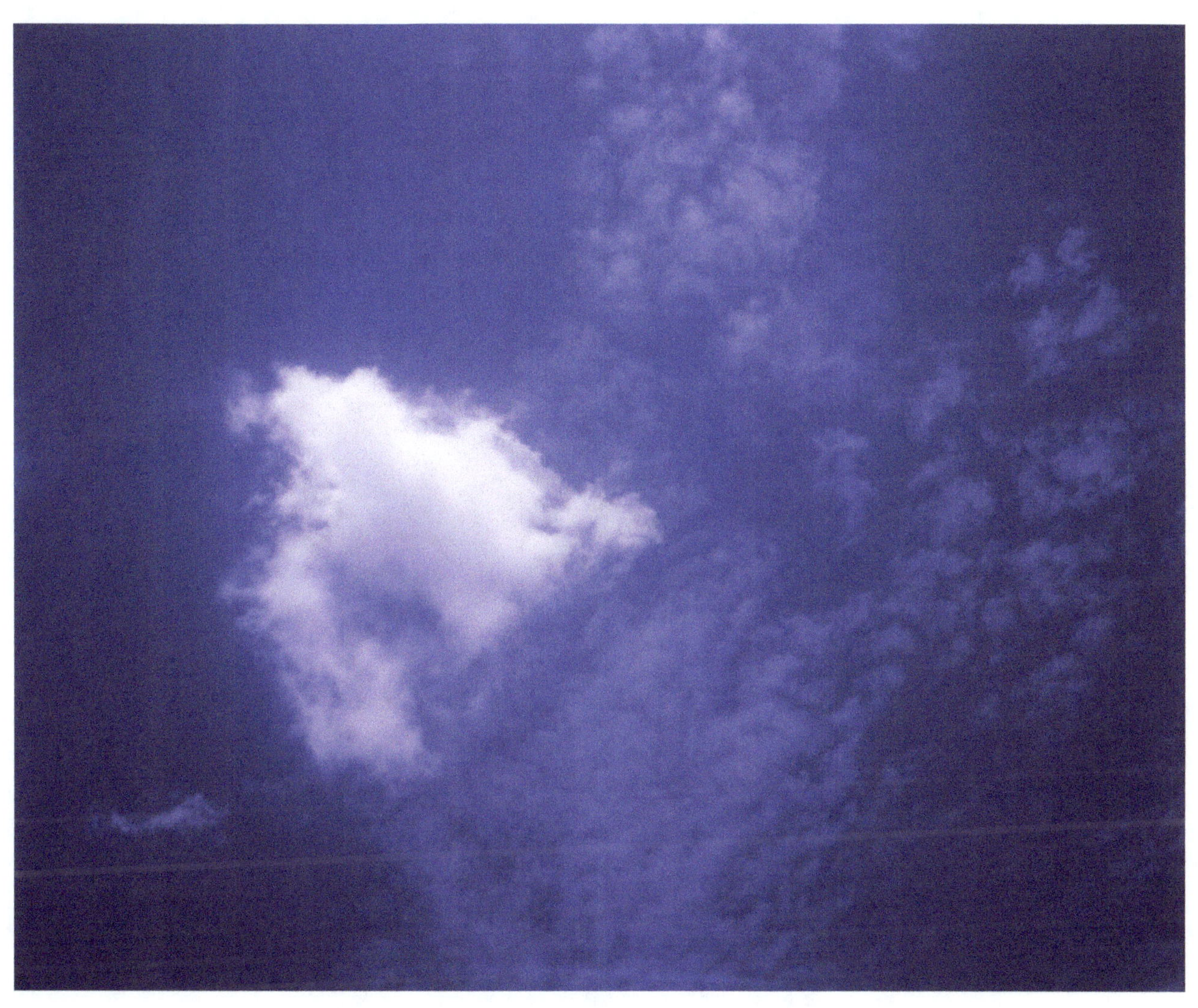

Spirit Dwelling

The face of tomorrow grows new opportunities of the future.

A première vue, le lendemain amène des nouvelles pour le futur.

Kristen, age 15.

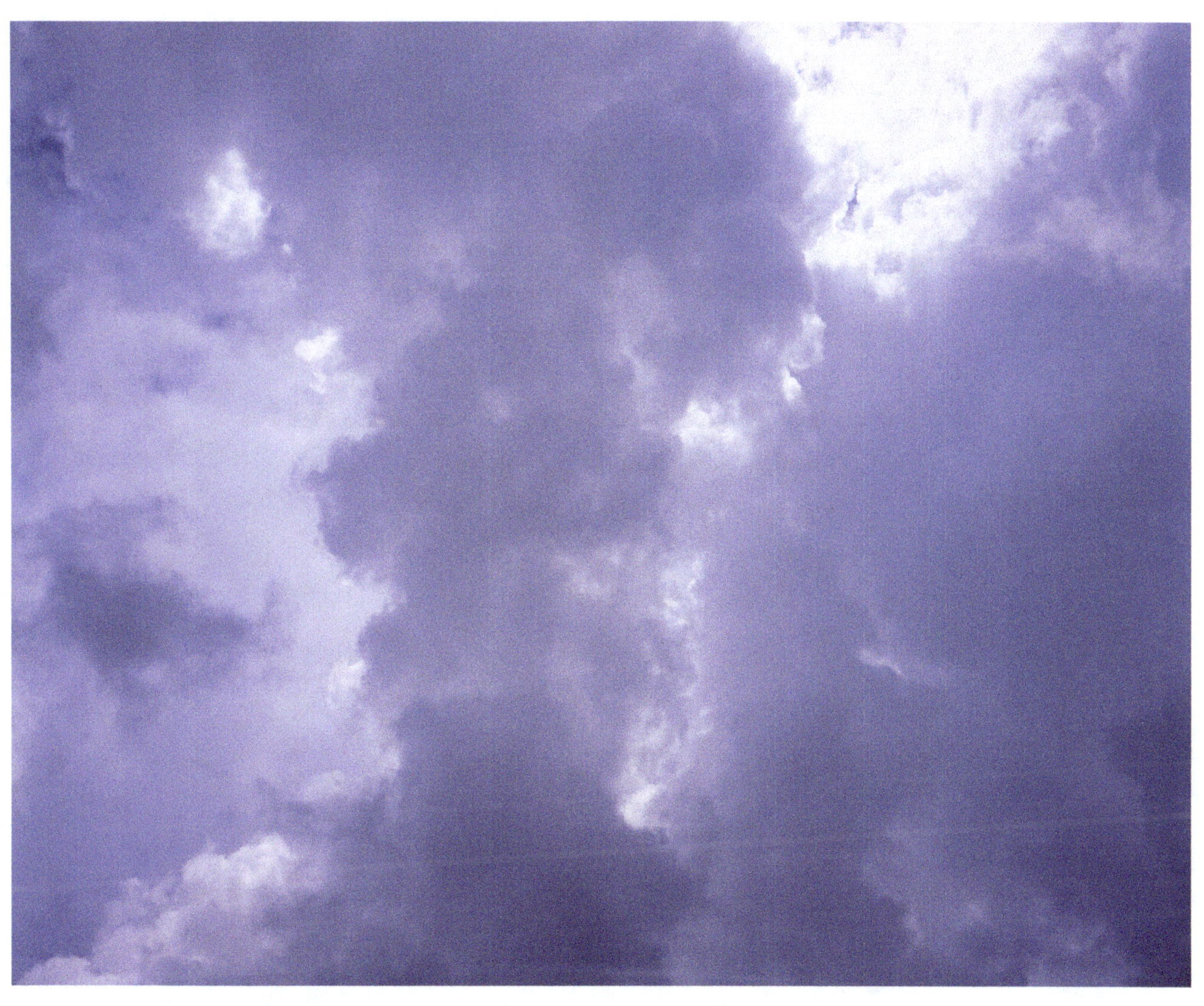

The Future

Love is something that comes in many shapes and sizes.
It can be a simple act of kindness
or even a feeling shared between two people.

L'amour se présente sous beaucoup de formes et de tailles.
Cela peut être un acte simple d'amobilité ou même
un sentiment partagé entre deux personnes.

Hanna, age 14.

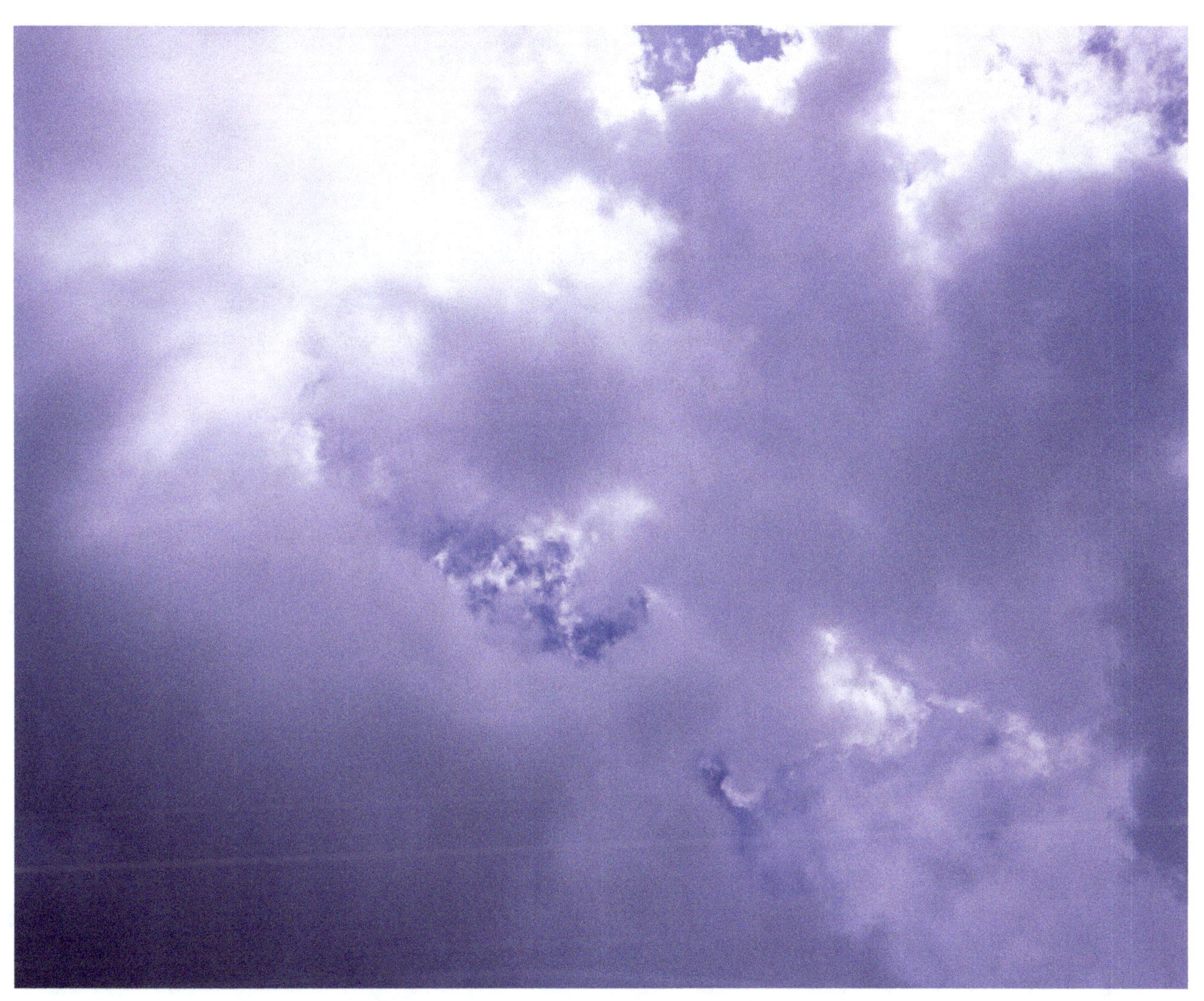

Healing Presence

You can always find the light, even in the darkest of storms.

Vous pouvez toujours trouver la lumière, même pendant les orages les plus sombres.

Emma, age 16.

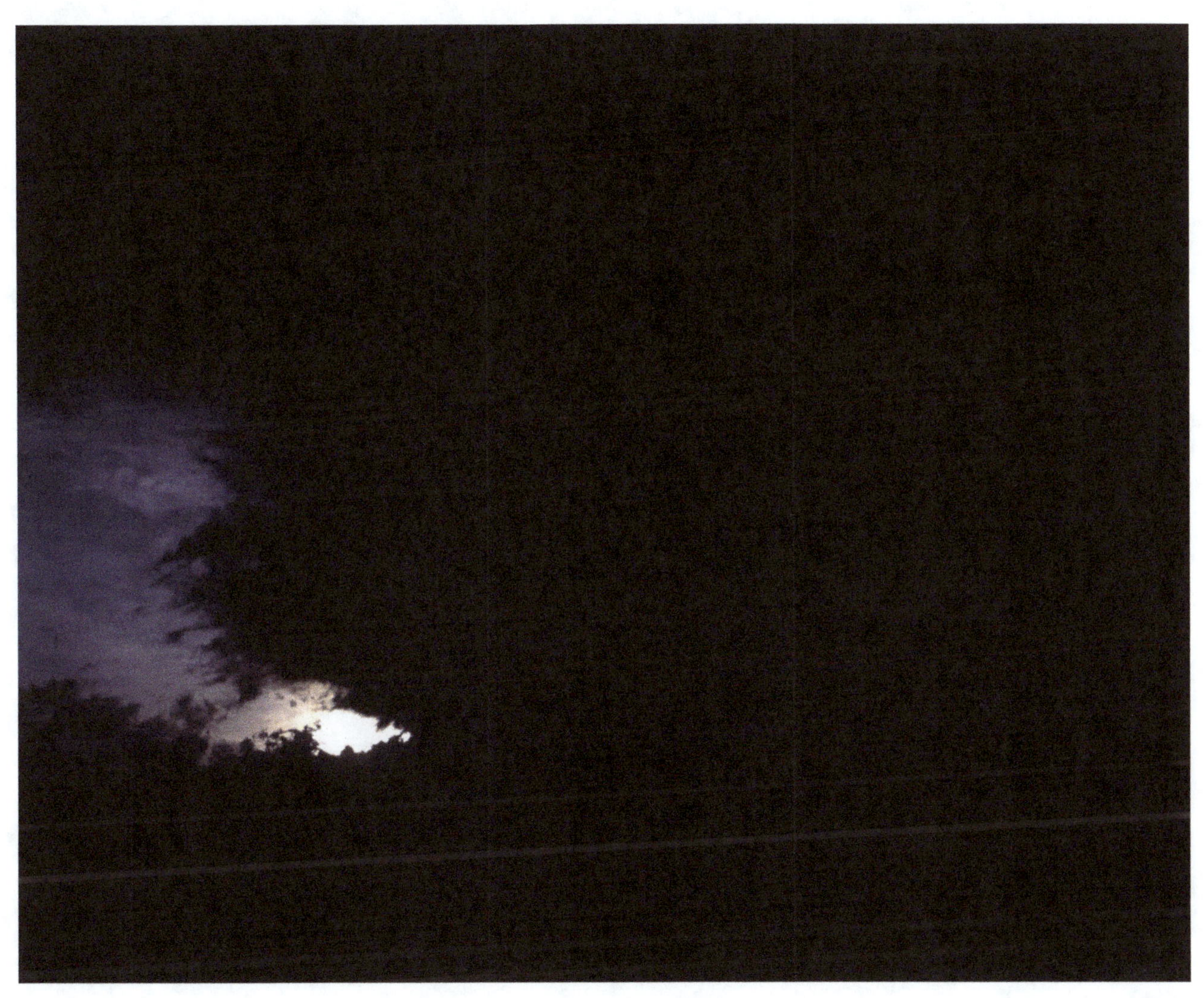

The Light Prevails

The sky is a mysterious object, always changing, never the same.

Le ciel est un object mystérieux, toujours changeant, jamais le même.

Michael, age 12.

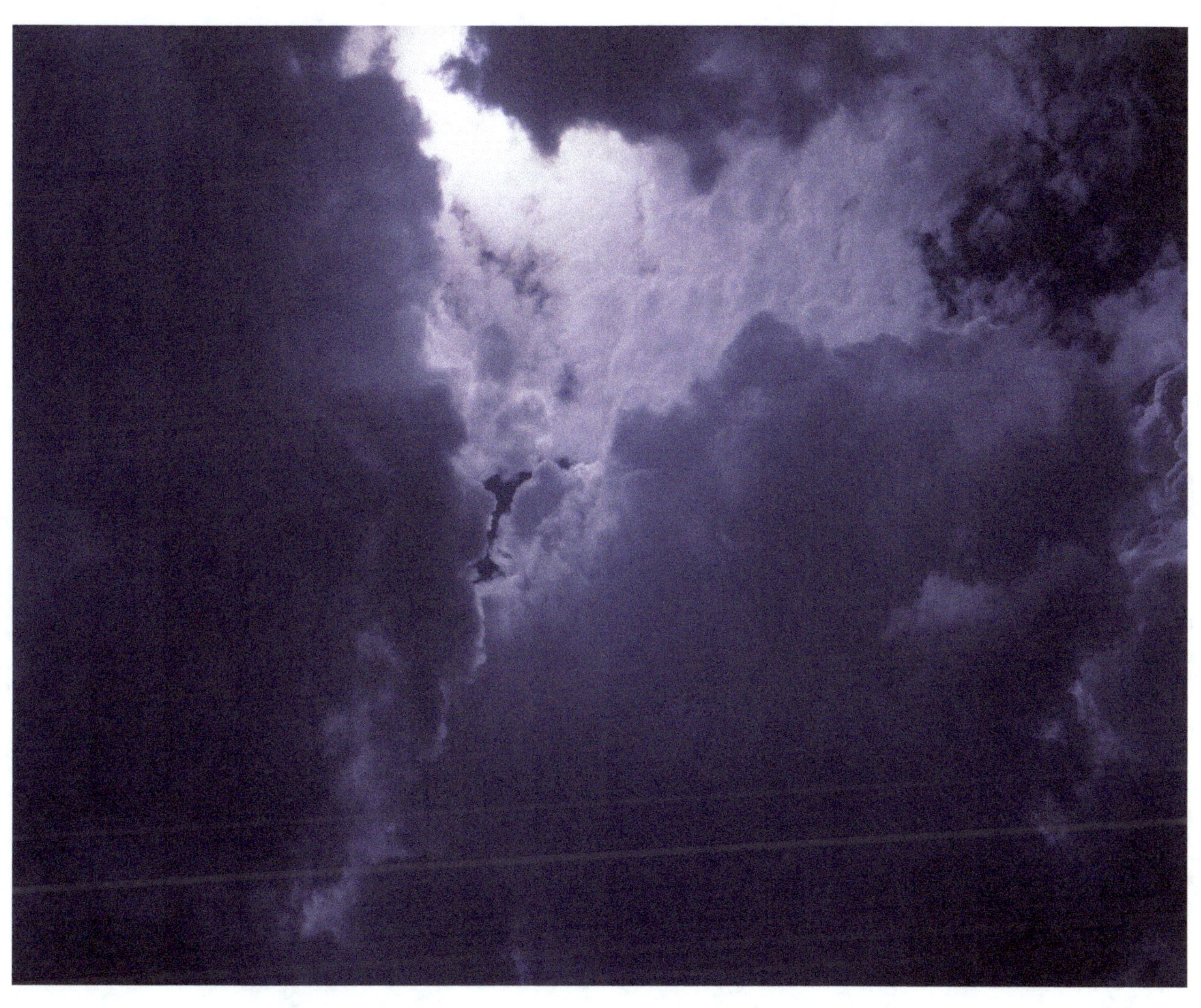

The Welcome

A thought is like a seed that God planted in you and is nurtured with courage, freedom, and happiness.

Une pensée c'est comme une graine que Dieu a planté en vous et qu' il nourrit avec courage, liberté et joie.

Annie, age 15.

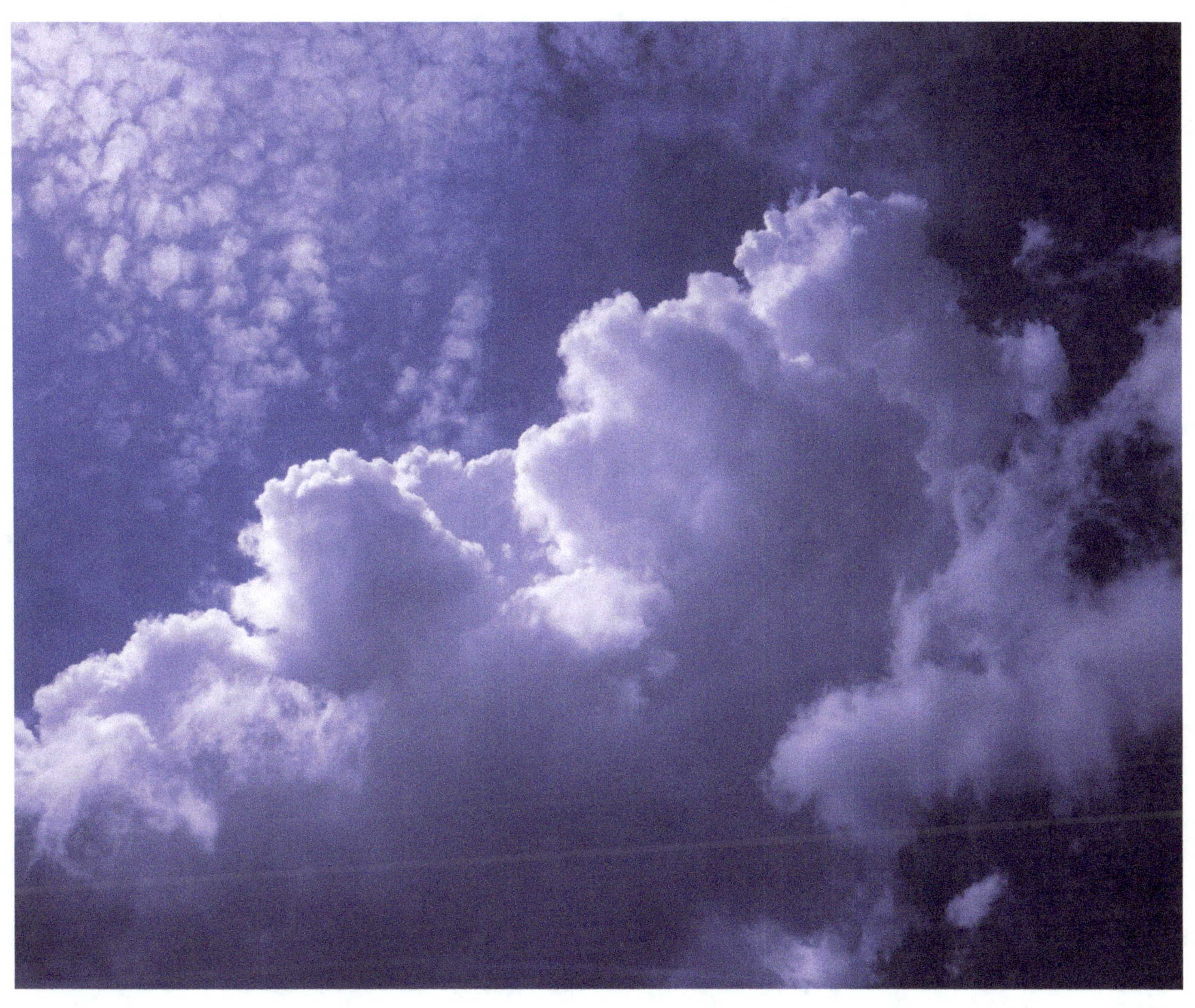

Thoughts Are Things

The sun is hot.

Le soleil est chaud.

William, age 5.

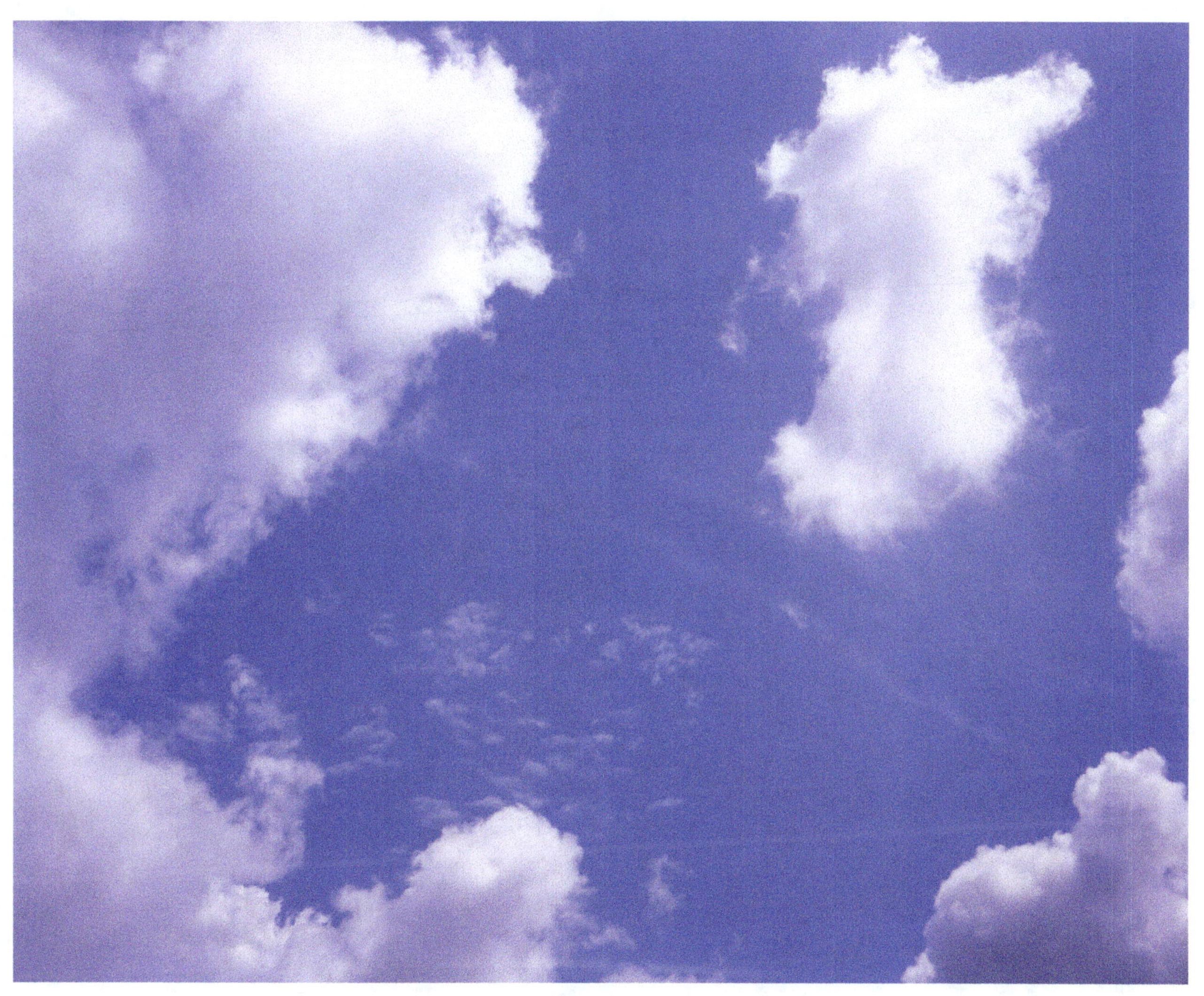

Up or Down

If I were a cloud,
I'd soar above the world,
With all the freedom I could imagine,
Just waiting for the wind to take me somewhere new.

Si j' étais un nuage,
Je m' élèverais au-dessus du monde,
Avec toute la liberté que je pourrais imaginer,
En attendant que le vent m'emmène quelque part inconnue.

Rose, age 12.

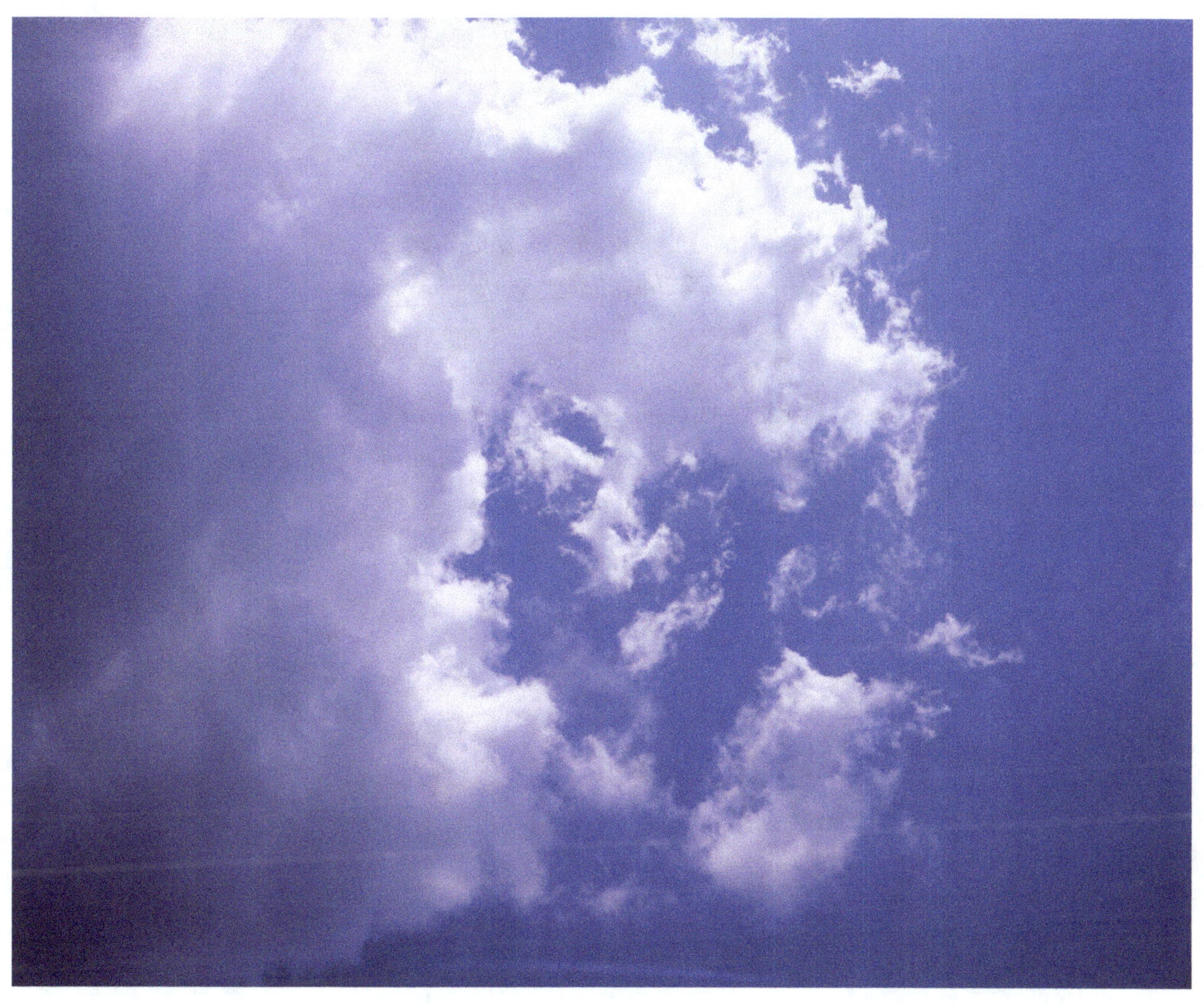

Wellness

God is the eyes that are always watching over us,
the hands that always comfort us,
and the everlasting love that fills our hearts.

Dieu est les yeux qui nous surveillent,
les mains qui nous réassurent, toujours,
et l'amour éternel qui remplie nos coeurs.

Katie, age 16.

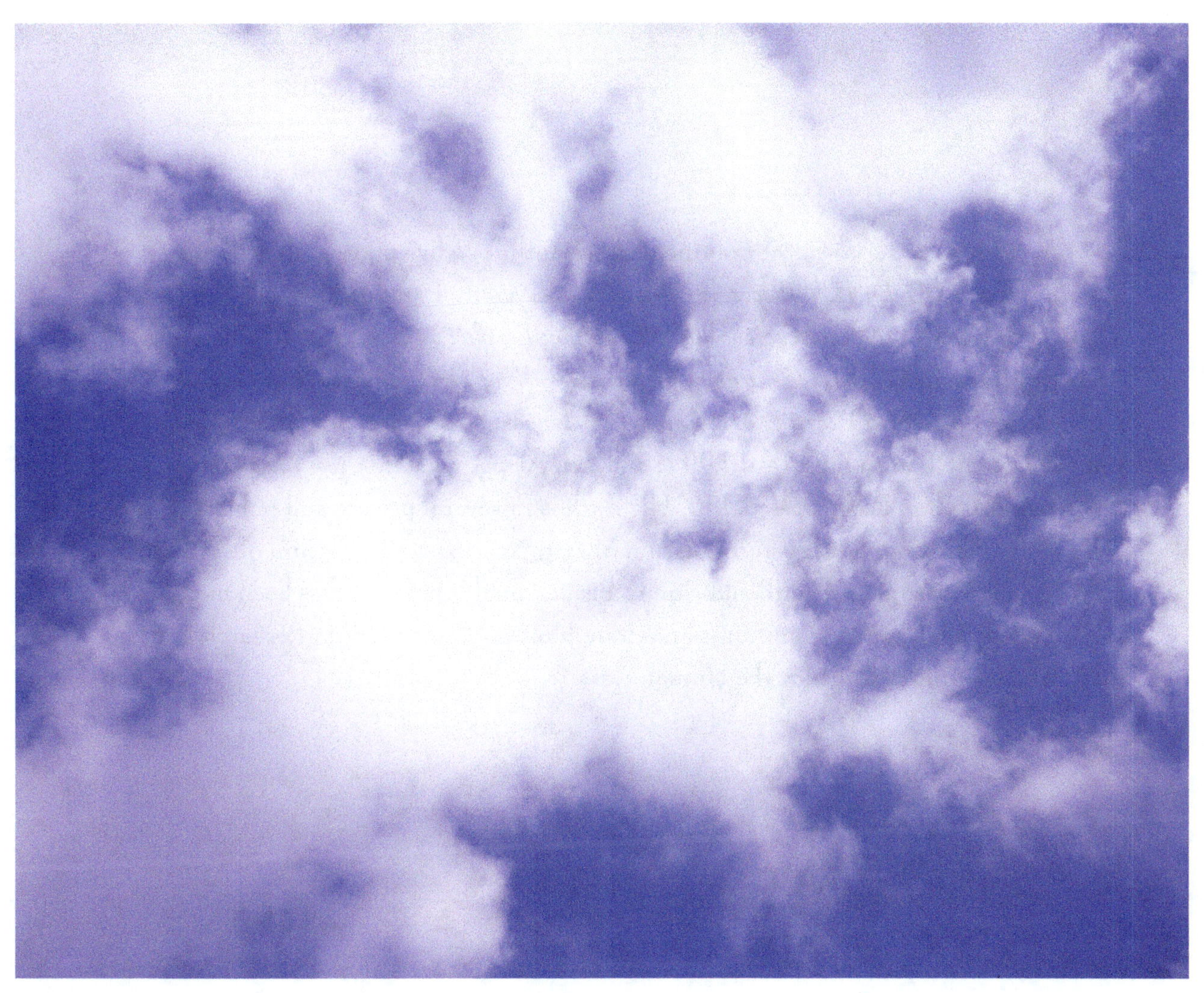

Guardian

A. J. Meek is the co-author of one and the author of five photography books including *Sacred Light: Holy Places in Louisiana*, University Press of Mississippi, 2010. Other books include *Clarence John Laughlin: Prophet Without Honor*, University Press of Mississippi, 2007; *Gettysburg to Vicksburg: Five Original Battlefield Parks*, University of Missouri Press, 2001; *Gardens of Louisiana: Places of Work and Wonder*, Louisiana State University Press, 1997; and *Red Pepper Paradise, Avery Island, Louisiana*, Audubon Park Press, 1986. His work is in several private and public collections including the Houston Museum of Art, New Orleans Museum of Art, and the Chrysler Museum of Art. In addition to his personal honors, he has been awarded several prestigious grants from Louisiana State University Council on Research and the Louisiana Endowment for the Humanities.

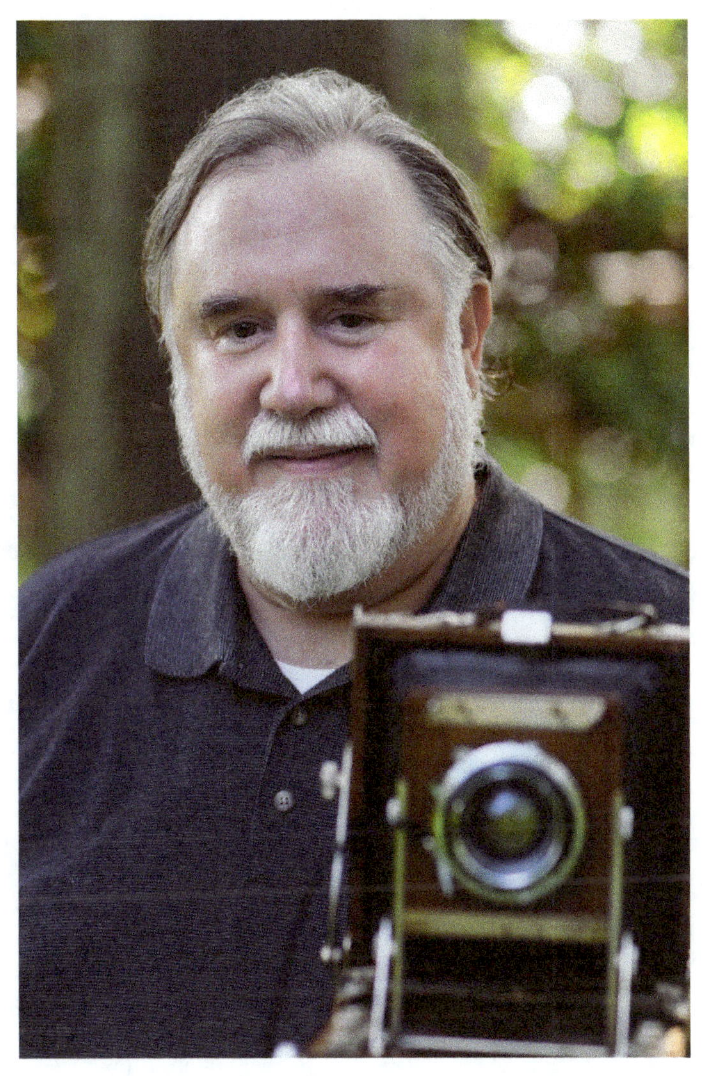

A. J. Meek with Camera (Photograph by Jim Zietz)

www.ingramcontent.com/pod-product-compliance
Lightning Source LLC
LaVergne TN
LVHW081253100826
845148LV00009B/1212

* 9 7 8 0 8 6 5 3 4 0 3 2 9 *